FANTASY CLIP ART

Everything you need to create your own professional-looking fantasy artwork

FANTASY CLIP ART

Everything you need to create your own professional-looking fantasy artwork

Kevin Crossley

**Andrews McMeel
Publishing, LLC**

Kansas City

Printed in China.

For information, write to:
Andrews McMeel Publishing, LLC.,
an Andrews McMeel Universal company,
4520 Main Street,
Kansas City, Missouri 64111

07 08 09 10 11 CTP 10 9 8 7 6 5 4 3 2 1

ISBN-13: 978-0-7407-6552-0
ISBN-10: 0-7407-6552-3
Library of Congress Control Number: 2006937913
www.andrewsmcmeel.com

This book was conceived, designed, and produced by
THE ILEX PRESS LIMITED
Publisher: Alastair Campbell
Creative Director: Peter Bridgewater
Editorial Director: Tom Mugridge
Editor: Adam Juniper
Art Director: Julie Weir
Designer: Ginny Zeal
Design Assistant: Kate Haynes
Commissioning Editor: Tim Pilcher

Artwork by Kevin Crossley, except Male Dwarf (p. 82),
Female Dwarf (p. 86), Male Child (p. 90), Female Child (p. 92),
Horseman (p. 94), and Horsewoman (p. 96) by Emily Hare.

Thanks to Liam Sharp for the guidance, Emily for her great
work, and Tom, Adam, and Tim at Ilex for all their great work
and help! Finally, a huge shout out to the Mam Tor posse,
without whom none of this would be possible!

CONTENTS

INTRODUCTION

It might seem that Fantasy is a relatively recent development in the history of art, but it has, in fact, been practiced by painters and illustrators since the very beginnings of mankind's artistic endeavors. Thirty-thousand-year-old cave paintings depicting heroic hunting exploits may be vastly different in style to the art we are familiar with today, but the themes they deal with are every bit as incredible and fantastic as the images found in contemporary posters, comics, and book jackets.

Egyptian hieroglyphs dating back five millennia often recount the journeys of kings from Earth to the heavens, or their transcendence from mortality to godhood, and the ancient civilizations of Greece and Rome are each steeped in artistic representations of their heroes and gods engaged in all manner of toils and adventures. Such subjects might well sound familiar, as they form the template for many Fantasy tales that have appeared over the past 50 years—whether the authors realize it or not!

Modern Fantasy Art, then, is no facile, fleeting fashion or fad; it is the latest step in the ongoing progression of a longstanding and well-established art form developed by artists through the ages. A common factor that links all of these disparate people throughout history is imagination. Imagination is part of what defines us; it drives our creativity and pushes us forward in our various quests to better ourselves or our societies.

Fantasy Art has always been about giving free rein to our imagination; this is as true today as it ever was. As a Fantasy artist you have the freedom to create whole worlds and populate them with hosts of amazing people, tribes, and creatures, then dream up swarms of monsters and beasts to do battle with heroes in fabulous environments. The possibilities are endless! This ability to make the unreal real is at the heart of great Fantasy Art, and this book is the perfect starting point to help you create your own fantastic characters and worlds.

Fantasy Art is all about escapism—everyone needs to lose themselves from time to time, whether in a good book, a film, or a graphic novel. What we regard as Fantasy Art these days often involves heroic warriors, battling maidens, elves, monsters, dragons, sorcerers, and noble kings populating strange realms where impossible events take place as though they were mundane and normal. This is the type of Fantasy Art we are concerned with in this book, and with the help of the tutorials in the first section and the ideas for characters and environments offered in the latter sections—together with the artwork contained on the CD—you will have all the tools you need to build whole new realities in which to escape!

INTRODUCTION TO THE DISC

The CD and book are two parts of a complete whole, neither complete without the other. The disc contains the computer files, but the book has all the know-how. For example, when you slip the CD into your computer, it will not take over your computer or direct you to run certain software. Instead it simply contains the graphics files—in the standard layered Photoshop format—contained within a simple folder structure you can access using the Finder (Mac) or Windows Explorer (PC). More likely, however, you'll want to start up your favorite layers-friendly graphics application and load the files you want via its *File > Open* command. The CD directory structure is explained opposite.

Over the following pages you'll find lots of examples of the different characters that can be created using those files. As you'll see, there are many illustrations within these pages, but they barely scratch the surface of the vast number of variations possible! A wide range of different creatures, characters, and subjects are presented in various different styles. Some are fairly simple, with bold outlines and limited detail. Others are more complex, with elaborate line work and textural shading already added. Whatever your skill level, artistic ability, or preference, you will find the perfect character to begin your Fantasy creations: From Barbarian warriors and ethereal Elves to lumbering Ogres and vicious Orcs, there are characters and creatures here to suit every aspiring Fantasy artist.

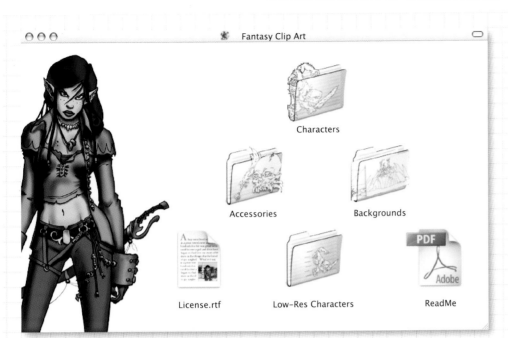

Fantasy Clip Art

Characters

Accessories

Backgrounds

License.rtf

Low-Res Characters

ReadMe

Characters
The meat of the disc—a folder of 25 axe-wielding, magic-casting, fantastic layered PSD files. Open them, turn layers on and off, and create one of thousands of possible characters.

Low-Res Characters
If you have an older computer, high-resolution graphics can sometimes slow things down. Let your computer keep pace with your creativity with these high-speed files.

Accessories
Add more personality to your creations with extra swords, spears, hats, and more. These can be positioned anywhere you like on your image using the techniques described on pages 20 to 21.

Backgrounds
If you want to design a complete fantasy environment, you'll need a setting for the action. Choose from eight customizable backgrounds, also supplied as layered PSD files.

Read Me
If you're worried you won't be able to use the layered files supplied, this file will direct you to Adobe Web sites from which you can download free 30-day tryouts of Photoshop and Photoshop Elements.

The Next Level
After you've spent some time creating your own unique characters using the art on the disc, you may feel that you'd like to experiment a little more. Why not try mixing elements from different character files to create truly bizarre and utterly fantastic creations? An Elf with an Orc head, for example! Perhaps you'd like to see what an Ogre looks like with Dragon wings? Or how about attaching a Barbarian torso to a Horse body to create your own Centaur warrior? The possibilities are almost infinite, and that's just the start! In time you might like to create your own character elements—design your own cool weaponry or costumes and mix them with the art supplied on the CD. As your confidence and Photoshop skills develop, you may well begin to create your own completely unique characters from scratch. Either way, your journey toward that goal begins with this book and the artwork supplied on the accompanying disc. Together they have everything required to feed your enthusiasm and drive your imagination through the clouds and beyond. The only question you will have to consider is how far can your imagination go?

DIGITAL FANTASY

INTRODUCTION TO DIGITAL ART

The use of computers in the production of art has revolutionized the way artists work and has made it very easy to create professional-quality images. Fast and powerful computers are already a fixture in many households, and art-focused peripherals have become incredibly popular. This, combined with improvements in software, has made it easier than ever to create superb Fantasy artwork.

Computers such as those shown here are capable of many things—storing your music library, editing your videos, and, most significantly from our perspective, editing images. There has been a great deal of development in that field recently, and we can use the results—powerful applications like Photoshop—to our advantage. You may already have access to most, if not all, of the equipment shown. If not, it can all be acquired relatively cheaply. Even Photoshop itself is now available in a cut-down form called Photoshop Elements. For the purposes of this book, everything can be achieved with this considerably less expensive program. Elements will also show you the color-coded layers we've used to make the creation of characters as easy as possible, though it won't let you change the color codes. From a professional perspective, the CMYK facilities and masking tools in the full version of Photoshop are invaluable, but at home you'll be able to draw, color, and have fun with either.

Mouse

Every computer has a pointing device, but it is worth making sure you have a good one if you intend to use it for artwork. Ideally, you should use a laser- or LED-based mouse. These are much more precise than traditional ball-based mice, and won't jam or become slow. Their other advantage is that they don't require such frequent cleaning to operate reliably. The only drawback is that they can be a bit picky about the surface they operate on.

Graphics Tablet

Although it takes a little practice, it's much easier to draw and color on a computer if you're using a graphics tablet. Many different brands and types of tablets are available. When buying a tablet, consider the software that is bundled with it, and whether or not the pen requires batteries. Although some popular brands can be more expensive, their quality and reliability can more than justify the cost.

Inkjet Printer

Color printing is now very cheap and high quality, and it's certainly worth having a color inkjet to see your creations on paper. Even relatively cheap printers are able to create good-quality prints, and quality can be improved considerably with the use of photographic paper (so long as you set the appropriate options in your printer's software). It's worth knowing that certain colors will look different when printed than on a computer screen. Many shades of purple will look different in print, as well as bright shades of blue and yellow, but your pictures will look great regardless of this small inaccuracy.

Laser Printer

Although laser printers—particularly the more affordable ones—are usually only black and white, they do have some advantages over inkjets. The lines are often crisper and the printing speed is significantly faster. Most importantly, the ink from a laser printer is waterproof and alcohol resistant. This means that printed pages can be handled without risk of being smudged by fingers, which is great for comic pages. It also means that it is possible to use markers to color in your characters, without risk of the ink smudging. Inkjet inks would mix with the pens and run. (One way around this is to use a photocopy.)

Internet

The Internet has made it much easier for artists to share their work than ever before. By publishing your artwork on the Net, you can get immediate feedback and comment from other artists. It's also possible to get advice and support when trying to improve your skills. Looking at other people's work can be both inspiring and informative when learning skills like computer coloring, and it's often possible to ask artists questions about how specific illustrations were made. Be sure to make the most of this great resource and allow the whole world to see your fantastic creations.

PHOTOSHOP AND PHOTOSHOP ELEMENTS

Photoshop has become the standard package for digital art among both home users and industry professionals. Although the software was originally designed for use in photo manipulation, the variety of tools it offers makes it the perfect choice for illustration, too. From an illustrator's perspective, and therefore that of a Fantasy artist, Photoshop offers flexibility combined with the ability to handle very high-resolution images.

Photoshop comes in two versions: the classic image editor, now part of the powerful Adobe Creative Suite; and Photoshop Elements, a cut-down version for home use. Both are ideal for our purposes. Let's see why.

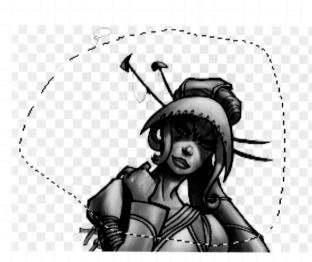

Selection Areas

When working in Photoshop, selections are an important way to control which part of the picture is affected by your painting. A selection is outlined by "marching ants" and changes can only be made within it while it is active. You can define a selection using tools—for example, the Rectangular Selection tool draws a simple box, while the Magic Wand tool selects areas of similar color, whatever the shape. When you have finished with a selection you must remember to switch it off, or "deselect," or you will not be able to edit outside it.

Layers

Layers are one of the most useful features of digital imaging. Imagine each layer is a piece of clear acetate with part of a picture drawn on it, creating the complete image only when the layers are stacked together. Because each layer can be manipulated independently, it is possible to work much more freely, without the risk of spoiling your artwork. You can use layers to experiment, simply turning them off if you don't like them, a process essential to building the fantasy characters in this book.

Tool Options Bar

While the Toolbox provides access to many different functions, the Tool Options bar allows you to refine the selected tool. If you're using the Brush tool, for example, you can pick different sizes and textures here.

Palettes

Both versions of Photoshop equip you with a number of floating windows, known as "palettes." Generally these palettes are docked against the side of the screen, but you can click on their names and drag them to the most convenient location.

Perhaps the most useful is the Layers palette, where you can switch on and off the alternative elements of the artwork supplied with this book. This is done by clicking in the box to the left of the layer. An eye logo indicates that the layer is visible, or "on."

Toolbox

The Photoshop Toolbox is the centerpiece of your digital Fantasy world. Without it you couldn't zoom in and out of your image, move your characters' accessories around, or paint them any color you wish. Here we'll have a quick look at the main tools in the Photoshop Elements Toolbox. (Photoshop itself has very similar tools, and the only ones we need to use appear in both versions of the program.)

Adobe Photoshop CS3 shown running on an Apple Mac Pro. If your computer has a large monitor (or two connected side by side), you'll find yourself with more room for your palettes. You can also zoom in and out of your image, but you should always check your artwork at 100%. That's because only at that size are the pixels in the file seen 1:1 with the pixels on your monitor. At other sizes, false pixels can create an inaccurate simulation of the final printout.

PHOTOSHOP TOOLS

While it's more than possible to fill entire books with details about using Photoshop, the program's core functions (and certainly the stuff we'll need) is easy to find. Whichever version of the program you're using, you'll need to be comfortable with the tools highlighted here.

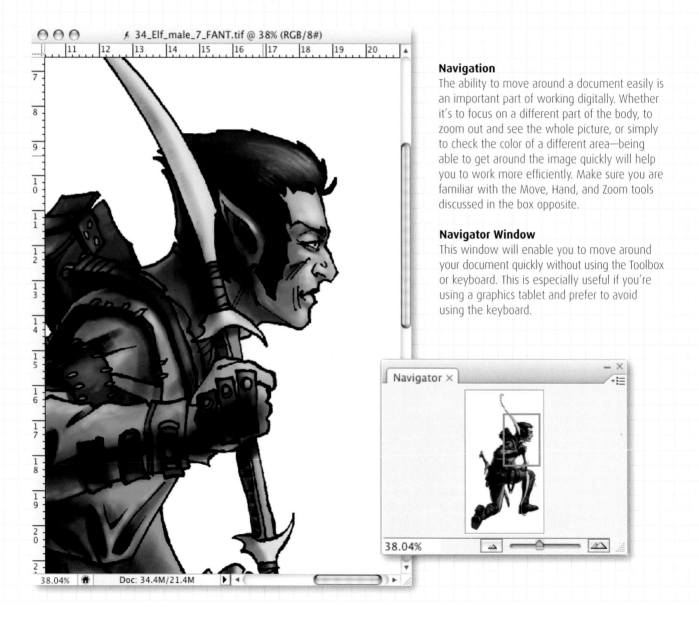

Navigation

The ability to move around a document easily is an important part of working digitally. Whether it's to focus on a different part of the body, to zoom out and see the whole picture, or simply to check the color of a different area—being able to get around the image quickly will help you to work more efficiently. Make sure you are familiar with the Move, Hand, and Zoom tools discussed in the box opposite.

Navigator Window

This window will enable you to move around your document quickly without using the Toolbox or keyboard. This is especially useful if you're using a graphics tablet and prefer to avoid using the keyboard.

Move
Click and drag to move the currently active layer or selection.

Zoom
Using the Zoom control will let you enlarge or reduce the preview of your image. Holding Ctrl/⌘ and pressing the + and – keys will allow you to zoom in and out at any time.

Hand
The Hand tool lets you pan (or scroll) the image around, making it possible to see different sections of the image.

Eyedropper
The Eyedropper tool selects any color you click on and makes it the foreground color (as shown at the foot of the Toolbox). Set the mode to "point sample" to ensure precise color picking. The Alt/⌥ key has the same effect when using the Brush.

Paint Tools
The paint tools are used to draw lines and add color to an image. Different shapes and sizes of brush will affect the way the lines appear on the image. See page 26 for more information on brushes.

Eraser
The Eraser deletes color from the currently selected layer. The Eraser works in exactly the same way as the Paintbrush, but removes the color instead.

Paintbrush
The standard painting tool, useful for soft edges and smooth lines. This is a great coloring tool, and there are many stylistic options in the Tool Options bar.

Pencil
A variation of the Brush tool, creating pixel-perfect (or "aliased") lines. These lines are very useful for cel-style coloring (see page 32), since by default the computer tends to soften edges.

Paint Bucket
This tool fills an area with a selected color, perfect for laying block colors on an illustration. Click on an area and it will be filled to its edges.

Selection
Accurate selections are vital for professional-looking artwork. Luckily, there's a tool for every situation.

Marquee tools
In both Rectangular and Elliptical form, these are the simplest selection tools, enabling you to highlight a simple rectangle or ellipse by clicking and dragging. Hold Shift as you do so for a perfect square or circle.

Lasso tools
These enable you to select any shape. The Freehand Lasso lets you quickly define a shape with the mouse, but is imprecise. The Polygonal Lasso works by drawing lines between a series of points.

Selection Brush
The Selection Brush allows you to "draw" the areas of selection directly onto the page. The Selection Brush is exclusive to Photoshop Elements, but Photoshop offers an alternative in the form of the Quick Mask feature, which allows other tools to be used to "paint" the mask.

Smudge, Blur, and Sharpen
These tools have no color of their own. Instead, the Smudge tool will smudge the colors around in the direction in which you move the cursor. Blur and Sharpen will alter the contrast of neighboring pixels to soften the definition, or increase sharpness.

Dodge, Burn, and Sponge
These brush-like tools adjust the color in different ways. Dodge lightens the color, while Burn makes the color darker and richer. These tools can offer easy ways to shade images, but most artists prefer to use layers and other methods of shading. The Sponge tool, on the other hand, absorbs the color and turns the image to gray.

CREATING CHARACTERS

Building a character from the files supplied on the CD is simple, with numerous possibilities. Let your imagination run wild and be sure to experiment with lots of combinations. The files have been designed to be as flexible as possible, so mix and match to create the best Fantasy characters you've ever seen.

1 Turn to the back section of this book—pages 49 to 121—and browse through until you see a character you would like to work with. There are 25 different characters, but each one can be altered to create numerous variations. Some of these variations are shown in that section of the book.

2 Insert the CD-ROM supplied with this book and open your graphics editing program. Click *File > Open* and locate the CD. Inside you'll find a folder full of named characters. From that folder, locate the file that corresponds to your choice of character from the book and double click to open it.

3 The image will load into your graphics program. You can now experiment with the layers and choose which ones will be part of your final image. The diagram opposite shows why this is important: With all the layers visible (or "switched on" as some people say), your character will be overloaded with multiple heads, limbs, etc. Select wisely (one head, one body, and a choice of accessories) and you've got a character. It's as simple as that.

Refining the layers
With all the layers turned on, the image is confused, but select just one head, one body, and some accessories and you can build a cool Fantasy character.

Nudging into position

With some of the more complicated characters, the heads, bodies, and accessories may not always line up precisely. In that case, choose the misaligned layer by clicking on it, select the Move tool, and either nudge the layer into place with the cursor keys or drag it with the mouse. Stop when you are happy with the new position.

4 To try different body parts and accessories, simply click on their visibility (eye) icons (at the far left of Photoshop's Layers palette). Here, for example, clicking on the Hair 1 layer switches on the long hair not seen in the previous step. A full listing of the layers available is shown at the beginning of each character's section, and all the examples have captions telling you which layers are used to create the individual image.

5 When you are happy with your selection of layers, save the image onto your computer using *File > Save As* from the menu. Don't worry, you will not be able to save over the original file on the CD-ROM. If your image hasn't ended up exactly as you'd hoped, try some of the following tricks to perfect your character.

Flipping

To get a whole new angle on your fantastic creation, try flipping the image. This can be applied at any time—before or after coloring—and is an ideal way to fit a second character into a scene when it doesn't initially seem to work. Simply click *Image > Rotate > Flip horizontal*.

Rotating or resizing

You may want to try rotating or resizing certain accessories—or even heads—to alter the appearance of your character. This is very easy to achieve using the Free Transform tool in Photoshop or Photoshop Elements. To rotate or resize, select the layer you wish to adjust in the Layers palette, then go to *Edit > Free Transform* (or use the keyboard shortcut Ctrl/⌘+T). A box will appear around the selected layer.

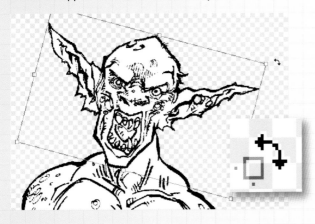

To rotate, hover the pointer just outside the box; it should change to a curved, two-sided arrow. Now click and drag to rotate the selection. (When doing this, you can also move the object by dragging inside the transform box.)

To scale, click and drag on the corner square (holding Shift/⇧ toggles proportional scaling).

Adding accessories

To add accessories to your character, open the accessory file alongside the character and narrow down your choice to a single layer (you will probably need to turn others off). Then simply drag that layer onto the main character image and close the accessory image again.

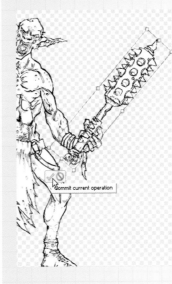

Position the accessory using the methods described previously. If necessary, reduce the accessory layer's Opacity temporarily and erase certain sections so that, for example, these fingers appear "above" the club.

6 To prepare the artwork for coloring, flatten the image to a single layer and make sure that no grays are present. Go to *Layers > Flatten Image*, then *Image > Mode > Bitmap*. Change the method to 50% Threshold. This means any shades above 50% darkness will become black, and any below will become white.

COLOR THEORY

There may be times when you've created the perfect character but can't finish coloring it because the hues just don't seem to work together. All you need in these cases is a little bit of knowledge about color theory. Once you understand some of the basic rules, you'll never need to worry about matching your colors again!

Primary Colors

In color theory there are three colors that cannot be formed by any combination of any other colors. These are the primary colors: blue, yellow, and red. From an artist's standpoint, all other colors we can see and use are created by mixing these colors in varying degrees (computer printers use the more technical cyan/ magenta/yellow).

Secondary Colors

These are the three colors achieved by mixing together the three unique pairs of primary colors: they are green, orange, and violet.

· To create green, blue and yellow are mixed together.
· To create orange, yellow and red are mixed together.
· To create violet, red and blue are mixed together.

These secondary colors have very interesting properties in relation to the primary colors. Each secondary color is composed of two primary colors, with one primary color left out of the mix. For example, orange is a mix of red and yellow, leaving blue aside. This means that orange and blue can both complement one another and repel each other. The same is true of yellow and violet, and red and green. These three partnerships can add balance to a composition if used carefully, but sometimes, if used insensitively, the results can be disastrous. Just see what sort of reaction you get if you wear a pair of purple pants with a yellow jacket. Sure, you may become the next fashion trailblazer, but you'll probably get a lot of incredulous looks first! So, experiment with these colors, both by themselves and against other colors; see how they work together, and more importantly, where they don't work. There are no definitive guides to which color combinations work and which don't—this is something you can only truly work out through your own explorations, so have a blast!

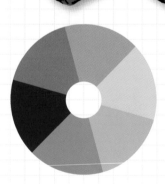

Tertiary Colors

Tertiary colors are those created when a secondary color is mixed with a primary color. There are six of these: red-orange, yellow-orange, yellow-green, blue-green, blue-violet, and red-violet.

The Color Wheel

The color wheel is a circular chart which represents the primary, secondary, and tertiary colors, and illustrates how they are related to each other. There are many variations of this wheel, some more complex than others, but what they have in common is their portrayal of a logically arranged sequence of colors, or "hues." The color wheel presented here is a relatively simple version, with twelve segments featuring the three primary colors, the three secondary colors, and the six tertiary colors. Take some time to study how the colors are arranged, and you will soon recognize the structured way in which they are laid out. It looks harmonious and balanced, with a natural progression around the wheel from any starting point. It is the essence of color harmony, and the simple rules it presents can be easily applied to your own work, resulting in colored art that is balanced and beautifully observed.

Color Opposition and Balance

This diagram shows the color wheel with a circular portion of the opposite hue placed inside each segment—the blue segment has a circle of orange within it; the red has a circle of green; the violet has yellow inside, and so on. The colors conflict with each other to such an extent that the diagram is quite difficult to look at. This diagram serves to illustrate the important and complex ways the colors within the wheel oppose and balance one another. See if you can get these combinations to work in one of your artworks!

BLOCKED-IN COLORING

Once your line art is prepared, one option is to block in the base colors for your picture. Filling in base colors creates areas of flat shading, much like many cartoons. It allows you to create characters quickly, or to experiment with the dominant shades you use in your picture. Choose these carefully, thinking about the kind of mood you want to create. Do you want to use lots of soft, pale colors, or strong, bold hues? The colors you choose now will affect the shading and highlights you add later, no matter which coloring method you choose to follow. Base colors create a foundation, or in some cases can be all the picture needs to look complete.

Before you begin
You might find that your line art is in monochrome, or Grayscale, mode. This means you will not be able to apply color. To solve this, go to *Image > Mode > RGB Color*. This enables you to use a theoretical palette of 16.8 million colors. Blocking in base colors is also much easier if you merge the layers first, by going to *Layer > Flatten Image*.

1 Prepare a character using the steps described on pages 18 to 21. Be sure to flatten the layers as shown, then save it to an appropriate location on your computer's hard drive using *File > Save As* (Ctrl/⌘+Shift+S).

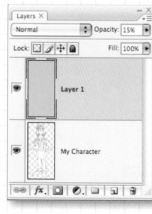

2 Rename your character layer if you like, then create a new layer above your character, and fill it with a pastel color at a low opacity (blues and greens are often best). Turning this on and off as you color will help make any gaps more obvious. This layer should be turned off when you have finished.

3 Create another new layer above the one you created in the previous step. In the drop-down menu at the top of the Layers palette, set the blending mode to Multiply. This layer will be used for colors.

4 Select the Paint Bucket tool, and make sure the settings have Anti-alias unchecked, Contiguous checked, and All Layers checked. Set the Tolerance to a small amount (such as 32) so that neighboring color areas are not filled accidentally.

5 With the base color layer you created in Step 3 active (highlighted), use the Paint Bucket tool to color each section of the image. Color the larger areas first, such as hair, skin, and clothes, leaving accessories and other details until later. This way you can make sure the colors used on the accessories will complement those on the clothes and hair.

Using the Color Picker
To choose a color, double-click on the color icon in Photoshop's Toolbox, click to choose a hue from the vertical rainbow-like bar, and the square will change accordingly. Now click anywhere within it to set saturation and shade.

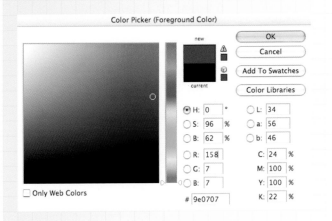

6 Continue to fill areas by clicking on them with the Paint Bucket. You can change the color you are working with either by clicking on it in the Toolbox or by opening the Swatches window.

COLORING AND SHADING WITH THE BRUSH TOOL

The Brush tool is a staple part of every Photoshop artist's repertoire. The opacity and flow can be adjusted to create a broad range of painting styles, and the brush shape itself can be altered and customized to create almost endless possibilities for interesting and varied brushwork. All in all, the Brush is a very powerful tool, intuitive to use, and an ideal place to start if you're new to digital art.

2 Select the Brush tool from the Toolbox (or press B) and tailor it to your purposes using the settings in the Tool Options bar at the top of the screen. To allow you to build up color slowly, set the Opacity to 50% and flow to 20%. New values can be entered directly into the fields or by typing a value on the keyboard (holding down Shift for Opacity).

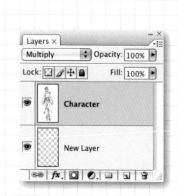

1 Create a Female Adventurer using the file on the CD. Flatten the image and save it to your hard drive. Create a new layer and place it beneath the line art. Set the blending mode of the character to Multiply—this allows any color in lower layers to show through the white areas, but not the lines.

3 Quickly block in the face and hands with an appropriate skin tone. The direction of the light source is something to consider at this point, and slight shading should be applied accordingly. (In this instance, the light is coming from above and to the right.) The strokes are careful, but loose, and it doesn't matter if they go over the lines, as this can be rectified later in the painting process.

Brush shape

Although the way you set your Brushes varies between different versions of Photoshop, the principles remain the same. A Brush can vary in size and in "hardness" (how dark the edges of the Brush are compared to the center). These can be modified using the drop-down menu that appears in the Tool Options bar when the Brush tool is selected. There may also be a button that brings out the Brushes palette. Here, many other attributes can be added—different textures, simulated hand jitter, and more. Experiment with these at your leisure—if you don't like the results, you can always press Ctrl/⌘+Z to undo.

4 Select a slightly darker color and reduce the Flow to 11%. Then paint over the shadow areas to reinforce them, accentuating the brightness of the light source.

5 Select a much lighter color with a hint of yellow for the lighter areas of the face and hands. Loosely paint these in to pick out the falling light a little more clearly. This process of working on a single section of the character is a good way to start. It enables you to become accustomed to the Brush while thinking about the light and shadow-fall in the piece. This can all be amended as the painting process continues, but it provides a good initial point of reference for the rest of the work.

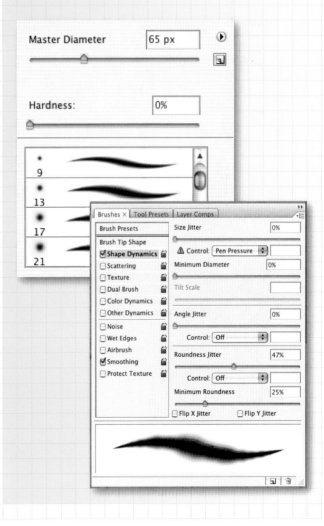

6 Paint in the rest of the figure, using broad strokes to establish the color scheme of the picture. Add some more subtle shading using lighter and darker versions of the colors you've already used.

7 Enhance the shadows even more with darker shades of the appropriate colors, adding extra weight to the picture. It doesn't matter if it seems too dark in places, as this can be tweaked and altered in later stages.

8 Ambient light can often suffuse shadows with subtle blends of reflected color. Use a soft red with the brush opacity set at a modest 25%, so that the color is gently applied to the darkest parts of the painting. Red is a good tone to apply to a dark or black area, as it adds depth and volume, even if used very lightly. Experiment with enhancing colors and shadows until you achieve the desired result.

9 To finish, pick out the highlights using lighter shades of the colors already chosen. This can include a little reflected light worked into the darker areas, creating a rounded illustration with weight and light. The brush strokes throughout have been loose and "painterly," adding plenty of movement and texture to the image.

USING LIMITED COLOR SCHEMES

Use of color in Fantasy art is obviously very important, but it can be quite daunting if you've had little experience with it or are unsure about which colors work well together. A great way to improve technique and confidence is to limit the number or range of colors you work with in any single piece of art. This approach not only removes some of the complications arising from working with disparate color schemes, but can help you achieve some quite stunning moods and effects, too, resulting in great colored artwork that is relatively painless to achieve. Here are some examples of artwork produced using limited color schemes.

Blue-Gray Troll

This troll character has been colored with gray tones subtly tinged with blue. Trolls are often associated with mountains or caves, and the gray hues suggest the creature's stony environment and skin texture. Blue is often used to color nighttime scenes, and as trolls traditionally rarely walk in daylight, using blue is the perfect way to suggest their nocturnal habits.

Ocher-Brown Orc

These colors can represent a dusty desert or a filthy environment, drained of color and life—just the sort of place you would expect to find an orc. Brown does have some subtle warmth in it, however, making it a very useful tone to use if you want to create dark areas of color without them appearing too lifeless or flat. Ocher hues expand the palette, offering tonal variation and contrast. These colors can also be useful in creating a feeling of antiquity or age in a project, and so are perfect for rendering scenes that might have happened long ago.

Red-Orange Dragon

These two colors represent heat and danger, the ideal color scheme for a dragon! Red is a powerful color; it jumps off the page and instantly draws attention to itself. Orange is a natural companion for red, offering a lighter tone where needed while losing none of the heat. A palette of reds and oranges can create an illustration that is larger than life, full of movement and rich character. It is also often associated with such disparate notions as nobility and monstrous evil, so it's uses are very broad indeed.

Yellow-Green Elf

Elves are associated with trees and so green is the natural choice when coloring these creatures. Green is soothing, creating feelings of calm and peace while retaining warmth and liveliness. Yellow is also a warm color and complements green perfectly—it is also lighter in tone and is perfect for portraying the skin and lightening the hair and other adornments.

SHADING AND HIGHLIGHTS

Adding color to a drawing is obviously a great way to add depth, character, and life, but color is just the beginning! Careful use of shading and highlights can really make your characters pack a visual punch.

| Begin by shading a picture using completely flat tones, as shown on page 24. This barbarian helmet is a good example—the simple colors are crying out for some light and shade.

2 The first step in shading is to decide where the light will be coming from: the direction of the light source. The position of the light in relation to the object will decide which areas of the helmet will darker and which will be lighter.

Tone

A great way to work out the tonal balance of a piece of artwork is to block in areas using just black and white. Using this method can tell you straight away how to light your work, and can look so cool as it is, that you might decide to leave it at that without adding any color at all!

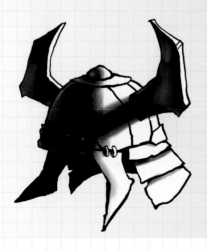

3 The light source is shining onto the helmet from the upper right, which means the left side of the helmet must be darker. With the Brush tool, apply slightly darker hues of the flat colors to the left side of the helmet. It immediately starts to look much better. This shading is then worked into the flat tones to create a smooth transition from the light to the dark portions of the helmet.

4 Next, consider not just the light source but the object's features, too, and add shadow-fall. The spike on the side of the helmet offers a dramatic example of shadow-fall which in turn, if painted strongly, will help to create the impression of a bright light source. Notice how the shadow cast by the spike merges into the shaded area on the left side of the helmet. Extra shadows are also added to indicate parts of the helmet that overhang other parts.

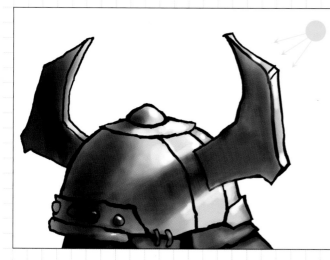

5 Now that the shading is done, it's time to think about highlights. Light is reflected in different ways from different materials, an important characteristic that can be illustrated perfectly by the helmet as it is made out of metal, which is very reflective, and leather, which is not so reflective. Careful application of the correct type of highlight can effectively and quickly differentiate between different textures and materials, and can serve to heighten the contrast between light and dark, essentially making the shadows appear darker. Use the brush to apply sharp highlights to the metal areas and soft, subtle ones to the leather parts.

6 The finishing touch is to add a little spot of ambient light: light that is reflected from other objects near it, or from the environment itself. Because it isn't as strong as direct light, it isn't visible in the brightly lit areas of the helmet, so you don't need to do anything to these. It does, however, manifest as a dull lightening within the shaded portions of the object. Choose a soft blue color and a very low opacity brush before painting the shaded areas. This adds a depth and fullness to these areas while not competing with the work so far. The result is a three-dimensional helmet that looks as though it is made of different materials.

ALTERNATIVE PAINTING TOOLS

If you're not familiar with the Brush tools in Photoshop, or you simply haven't had much practice, the prospect of painting can be daunting. However, Photoshop has many other methods of coloring that don't have to involve the Brush tools, and can be just as effective. Here, the Lasso tool is used to isolate areas of flat color, which are adjusted using the Hue, Saturation, and Lightness controls. Shading is then added using the Dodge and Burn tools to finish the image. This is a quick and effective way of coloring line art.

3 Click on the Lasso tool and use it to select the face and hands. Do this by drawing around them as if you were using a brush (click and hold as you move the mouse).

2 Create a single-color fill in the new layer beneath the Elf ranger character.

4 Bring up the Hue/Saturation dialog box by going to *Image > Adjustments > Hue/Saturation* (the menu command varies slightly in different Photoshop versions). Drag the Hue slider until you find a suitable skin tone, then adjust the Lightness slider until you achieve the desired result. As this is a Wood Elf, the skin tone is left slightly greenish.

1 Create a new layer and place it underneath the line drawing of the Elf ranger. Change the Elf ranger's blending mode to Multiply, which allows any color in lower layers to show though the white areas.

5 Using the Lasso tool, select each different area of the image in turn, and adjust the Hue, Saturation, and Lightness sliders until the entire character is colored. (If you find the Lasso tool too cumbersome, try selecting the different areas with the Magic Wand tool instead.)

6 The Elf is starting to look much better, but the colors are still very flat. The next stage involves adding shading using the Burn tool, so select it from the Toolbox. With the exposure set to 30%, lightly brush the Burn tool over the image to darken certain areas. Use it to create the impression of a light source (see page 32), in this case coming from the upper right. The strokes can be quite rough and loose, adding texture and character to the piece.

7 Switch to the Dodge tool. This tool is located next to the Burn tool, or in a subgroup with it, in the Toolbox. A few quick strokes on the upper right surfaces of the Elf are enough to strengthen the apparent light source, resulting in a convincing colored image that was relatively quick and easy to complete.

8 As a finishing touch, add a little ambient backlighting. Again, use the Dodge tool, but this time on the left (shade) side of the character, as if the light source is coming from behind him. This light is very subtle, so use the Dodge tool very lightly to enhance the solidity of the image.

REFLECTIVE PROPERTIES

Over the last few pages it's become clear that the principles of applying light and shadow to Fantasy images are grounded in the way real light behaves, in particular the direction it comes from in relation to the object it illuminates or casts into shadow. If, for example, the light source is from the left, it logically follows that the left side of the object will receive highlights, while the right side will be in shadow. This is a basic principle that if followed will result in a firm understanding of how to light your artwork effectively.

That is, of course, a simplified way of describing a subject that can become very complicated. When you are comfortable with basic applications of light and shade, it's worth thinking about how light alters depending on what sort of material it is illuminating.

The best way to learn more about how light works is to use your eyes. That sounds obvious, but we are so accustomed to the way the world looks that we rarely actually attempt to ascertain why it looks as it does. By observing shadows, questioning what is making them, and doing the same with illumination, you can learn far more than a book will ever teach you. Learn not just to look, but to properly *see*. Ask lots of questions, and the answers will soon be forthcoming.

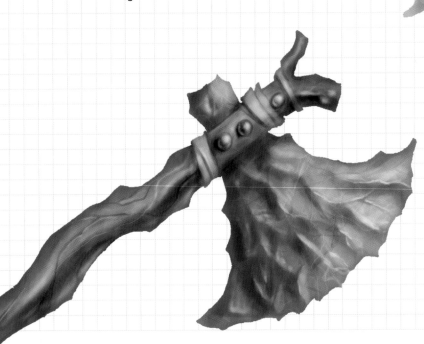

Polished helmet
Polished metal reflects a lot of light. The highlights are very bright as a result, and the boundaries between light and dark on its surface can appear very abrupt and stark.

Stone-age axe
Stone reflects light in many different ways, depending on what sort of stone it is and how it is shaped. A granular rock such as sandstone will not reflect much light, although upon closer inspection the surface may appear to sparkle with tiny points of light, like stars, as tiny grains of silica reflect the sunlight. Other types of stone, such as flint, are much smoother and sharper, and can shimmer as highlights enhance their edges and facets.

Leather

Fabrics and garments also vary greatly in their reflective properties, with materials such as silk or waxed leather being particularly shiny. However, many of the characters depicted in this book would probably be clothed in travel-stained, well-worn garments and armor, which would feature soft shadows next to subdued, diffuse highlights.

Evil skull

Of particular interest to the Fantasy artist, of course, is bone. Due to its off-white color, bone reflects a lot of light, but doesn't necessarily give off strong highlights. Due to its luminosity, any shadows around bone are heightened, making it a material of stark contrast against most other materials or backgrounds.

Furry monster

Another material that can exhibit bold highlights is hair or fur. If the hair is of uniform length, the highlight will take the form of a band or sheen of reflected light, but if the hair is tufty, like matted or scruffy fur, then the light will pick out the tips and points of any hair peaks or fibers that protrude from the overall mass.

COLORING THE COVER IMAGE

All artists develop their own methods, and I am no exception. For the color image used on the book cover, I began with a variant of the Adventurer character from the CD, and colored it using the following steps.

1 My first step was to apply a Hue/Saturation adjustment to set a basic color on which the character's color scheme could be based. To do this, the character layer—the lines themselves—were lightened using the Hue/Saturation dialog's Lightness slider. This turns the black lines to gray, which will allow color to be added later. Repeating the process but dragging the Lightness slider the other way darkens the white background areas of the character to gray, while leaving the transparent pixels untouched. Finally, color can be added to the work by going to *Image > Adjustments > Color Balance...* (Ctrl/⌘+B) and adjusting the sliders.

2 The flowing cloth of the costume was then blocked in using the Brush tool, with Opacity and Flow each set to 100%. The brush size was varied depending on the area being worked on (press [or] to increase or decrease the brush size while you work). I also worked out the basic shadows and highlights at this stage.

3 I set the Opacity and Flow of the Brush tool to 35% and built up a palette of colors on a separate layer, chosen from the major colors already in use. Using the Eyedropper tool (press Alt/⌥ if the Brush tool is selected) to select colors from this palette, I used the brush to softly paint away the obvious borders between the blocks of color. In some places the strokes are bold and broad, in others a smaller brush was chosen to apply specific detail. High detail was added using a very small brush with Opacity and Flow set between 60 and 95%. This ensures a fluid flow to the work, retaining energy and interest with occasional islands of deeper detail for the eye to linger upon.

4 Next, I repeated Step 2, this time blocking in the base colors for the rest of the character. New color swatches were created as this process progressed, building up an extensive palette of colors to pick from in the final stages.

5 As each area was worked on, I continuously altered the brush size to apply occasional spots of detail and add shadows and highlights along the way. The application and accuracy of the brushwork was continuously and deliberately varied; sometimes rough, expressionistic splotches of color were applied, giving way in a moment to highly focused, blended tonal work. Color was not restricted to tonally analogous areas; a little of the red might be applied to the armor, a little skin tone might find its way onto the leather. By mixing the colors this way, the whole piece is afforded a sense of continuity to complement its spontaneity.

6 I added a few finishing touches, such as bright spots of reflected light on the metallic areas and reflected ambient light in some of the shadows, and the painting was complete. It has color, texture, drama, movement, and dynamic composition— everything a good piece of Fantasy art should have!

SPEED PAINTING

As unlikely as it sounds, speed painting is perhaps one of the most difficult exercises to master, but it has the potential to yield huge rewards. Producing a series of speed paintings over the course of even a single day can help improve technique, accuracy, focus, and of course, speed. It can improve your practical knowledge of color theory, lighting, shade, tone, and composition as well as loosen up your muscles and stylus/brush grip, which in turn will produce a much looser, more exciting style of painting. In time, you'll be turning out painting after painting, and with each one you'll see an improvement in your work. You might even discover a few new techniques or ideas. The point of speed painting isn't necessarily to produce a finished piece of art, it is simply an exercise to unlock many of the mysteries surrounding painting technique. The ultimate challenge is to produce 15 paintings in a single hour . . . so, what are you waiting for?

Start
A worm-like creature is created using the Monster character file on the disc.

One minute
Color is quickly blocked in over the line art. The black line is changed to a darker red in the process.

Start
The last speed painting was fast, but this pushes it to the limits. Before the clock is started, a Fairy is constructed using the Child Female file from the disc.

2 minutes
A cheerful, bright green is painted roughly over the drawing using an Opacity of around 30%. Some consideration is made for the light direction, and darker shades are applied accordingly.

5 minutes
A pinkish skin tone is brushed onto the face, arms, and leg areas. The left side of these skin areas are left unpainted to give the impression of shadow. A lighter green and then yellow are applied to the whole character to boost contrast.

Six minutes
Using the Brush tool, a darker hue is painted over the base color to block in the shadows and define the light direction. Brush strokes are quick, broad, and loose.

14 minutes
The shaded areas are enhanced, and reflected light added. The brush strokes are left as applied, never once undone. It's better to identify mistakes and then paint over them.

28 minutes
A lighter hue is chosen and quickly daubed over the brighter areas. This is a good opportunity to enhance the texture of the different skin areas, making some shinier than others.

Finished
A final touch of soft blue reflected backlighting and the painting is complete! A completely repulsive slug/worm monster in just 43 minutes!

10 minutes
Darker green is now washed over the left part of the figure, and other shadowed areas are also enhanced. Close attention is paid to the face during this stage; the features are worked up, with highlights being added, particularly to the eyes.

17 minutes
In a final frenzy of brushwork, the edges of the character are darkened with bold strokes of dark, brownish red and a darker green. Light yellow-greens and pale lemon tints enliven the lighter tones, and the face is adjusted slightly. Stop the clock! Finished!

CREATING AN ARMY

One of the great benefits of Photoshop (or indeed any digital image editor) is the ability to create multiple copies of a drawing or element that can then be used to create new scenes or designs. The following tutorial will describe a simple process you could use to build an entire army using just one of the characters on the CD.

Now, obviously this makes for a rather strange army, made up as it is by identical Barbarians all moving at exactly the same time, but you can of course use the disc to create your own army of unique characters with which to populate your scene.

2 Paste a background into the layer behind to give the character something to stand on, and provide focus, depth, and space.

1 Create a Male Barbarian character using the file on the CD and color it. Next, we need to expand the area around the image. Select the Crop tool from the Tools palette (shortcut C) and click and drag a box around the entire canvas. Drag the handles to increase the amount of space around the Barbarian. This will be useful for the subsequent stages.

3 Move the Barbarian to the left of the picture, and reduce him in size using the Free Transform tool (Ctrl/⌘+T).

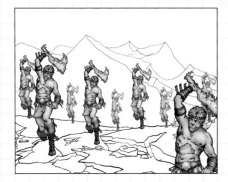

4 Be sure that the Barbarian layer is selected, then click *Layer > Duplicate Layer*. This creates a duplicate layer above the original. The duplicated Barbarian can then be placed anywhere else on the canvas using the Move or Free Transform tools. Use the Free Transform tool to scale him too, to make him appear to be a little behind the first Barbarian, and a little farther away.

5 Repeat this duplication and resizing process (always working from the large original Barbarian) until the scene is filled with an arrangement of Barbarians. Use different sizes to help create the illusion of an army positioned at various points in a three-dimensional environment.

6 Next, enhance the feeling of space by using the Lasso tool to select individual Barbarians, then blurring them. Once selected, click *Filter > Blur > Gaussian Blur*, then adjust the radius slider to achieve a slightly blurred affect. This works like a camera's depth of field, seeming to push characters into the distance, or make them seem closer than the "focus point."

7 Finally, apply a few tweaks here and there, such as removing the feet of the smallest Barbarians to make them appear as if they are behind the brow of the hill, and the scene is complete. You could now start painting the background.

GET YOUR HANDS DIRTY

As you become more and more familiar with the files on the CD, you might begin to wonder how the actual files were created, perhaps to help you create new parts for the characters, or even to design entirely new ones yourself! Here I will show you some of the steps I took when designing the Female Elf character.

1 The first step involves producing a quick sketch to work out a basic framework which will in turn be used to create the character variations. Quite often such a sketch is done using pencils or ink pens, but in this case a loose digital sketch was created in Photoshop. Blue is used rather than black, as this will simplify the job of tidying up the drawing after the inking has been applied.

2 The digital sketch is printed out onto paper, and a black ink drawing pen is used to follow the sketch to create a finished template—a standard Elf female character which will form the basis of the rest of the work to come. A few weapons are also drawn in, just to get the process started. The version shown here is presented with the blue digital under-drawing removed in Photoshop.

3 Next, tracing paper is placed over this first ink drawing, and blue pencil is used to design a number of different bodies, legs, heads, and costume variations, each being drawn directly over the ink drawing to ensure they all match up when the digital PSD file is constructed. Blue pencil is used for the same reasons as before.

4 A black ink drawing pen is utilized once more to create strong line versions over the top of the blue pencil art. Sometimes the line work is basic and simple, but sometimes more complexity is required to create different moods for certain types of characters. This can be quite a laborious procedure, but can be very rewarding when finished.

When the ink work is completed, all the inked art is scanned into Photoshop. The software is used to eliminate the blue art, resulting in clean black-and-white line work. The lines are strengthened where required, and any spots or blemishes are removed. This will make sure the white background areas that surround the character elements can be easily removed before the last stage is carried out.

5 The final stage is the most time consuming. Each area of the character—head, body, legs, weaponry, and other adornments—must be broken up, cut out of their layers and pasted back into the file on their own layers. Each separate layer is named appropriately and arranged in an order that will make it easy to construct

any number of variations. The Female Elf character turned out to be quite complex, more so than many of the other characters, so she turned into two separate PSD files, each one capable of creating numerous unique versions of the character. Here are just a few examples of the different Elf female variations which are possible.

EVOLUTION OF THE SPECIES

By now you've no doubt spent many happy hours locked in your room experimenting with the files on the disc. Perhaps you've created the beastliest Orc or the biggest Barbarian brute ever seen! Maybe you pieced together a Dragon that was so terrifying you had to leave the room and cower in the cupboard under the stairs for a while. That's all great, but now it's time to push the limits of your imagination even further. Like the sensible motorist, it's time to look at hybrids.

Your character development needn't be constrained to using the layers from a single file. Open up a few different character files from the disc, choose layers from each one, and paste these into a new file to form the basis of the next generation of incredible characters or creatures.

Although wild and monstrous, these are still relatively tame compared to the possible hybrids that could be created if you went *really* nuts! A good method of measuring the weirdness of your creations is to show them to a well-adjusted member of your family or a passing person in the street. The ideal reaction should be anything from mild disbelief as they attempt to decipher what it is they're looking at, to wild screaming followed by running away. If you can make that happen, you *know* you're in the right ballpark!

Elf Monster
Try taking an Elf female body and attaching it to some of the Monster parts. Pretty bizarre, eh?

Ogre Centaur
How about mixing parts from the Ogre with those of the Horse to create this grisly Centaur?

Reality Plus

If you look at animals and people, you'll notice their physical structure is constructed with certain principles and natural balances in place. For example, most mammals and lizards have two forelimbs or arms, two hind limbs, one head, a rib cage, etc. However, your warriors don't need to adhere to this notion. Try adding extra limbs or heads, scatter a few extra eyes around the body, give them more mouths, or remove other features altogether!

Practical Insanity

Although in Fantasy art anything should be possible, you might like to balance the suspension of disbelief with a little common sense. For example, if you want to sell the idea of a Barbarian with seven arms, it's probably best not to weld them all onto its head. How would the bones attach? How would the muscles function? In such a situation they would most likely hang limply down around the shoulders like a horrific wig; not a favorable look for any self-respecting Barbarian about town. It's better to attach such extra limbs to places on the body that would appear more able to support them . . . *if* you care about that sort of thing, of course! After all, these are all just suggestions. This is *your* book, and you should feel free to let your imagination off the leash to run in any direction it chooses!

CHARACTERS

MALE ADVENTURER

The male adventurer has 22 layers, with a wide variety of poses available. There are two sets of legs, with five different upper bodies. Three of the upper bodies are unique poses with heads attached, but the remaining two can be used with any of the six heads also supplied.

Layers

	Upper body 5
	Upper body 4
	Bag
	Upper body 3
	Head 6
	Head 5
	Head 4
	Head 3
	Head 2
	Head 1
	Upper body 2
	Upper body 1
	Legs 2
	Legs 1
	Scabbard
	Axe
	Arrows
	Box
	Sword
	Step 3
	Step 2
	Step 1

Axe Warrior

	Upper body 5
	Legs 2
	Axe
	Step 2

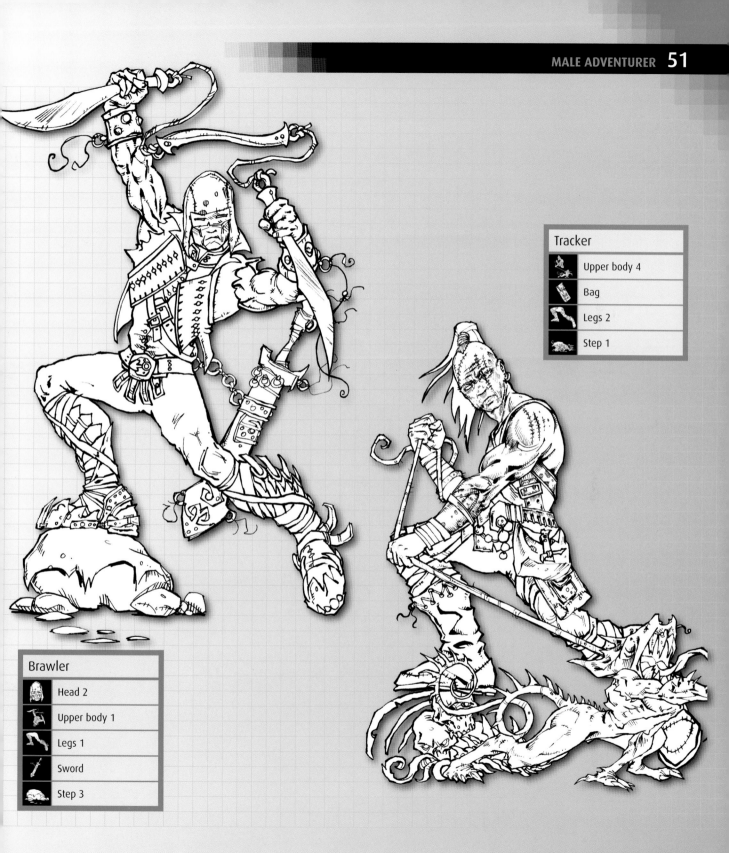

Tracker

	Upper body 4
	Bag
	Legs 2
	Step 1

Brawler

	Head 2
	Upper body 1
	Legs 1
	Sword
	Step 3

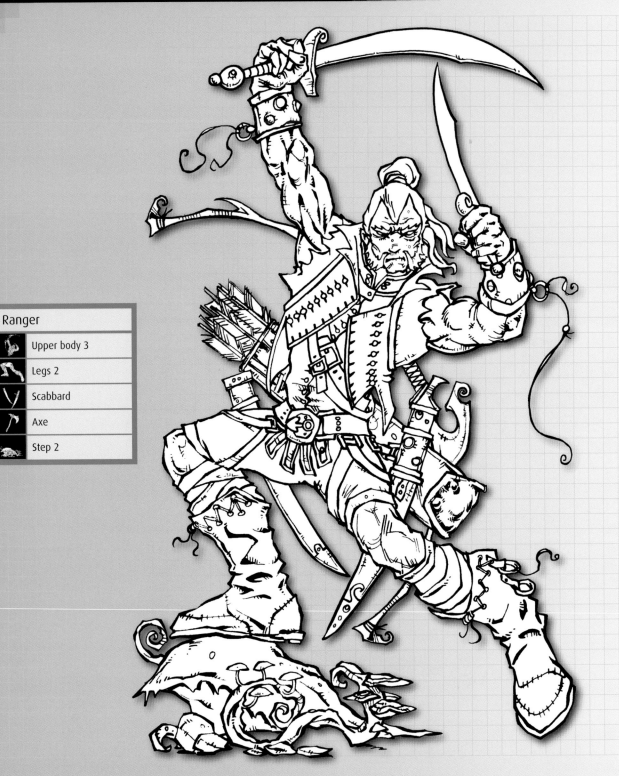

Ranger	
	Upper body 3
	Legs 2
	Scabbard
	Axe
	Step 2

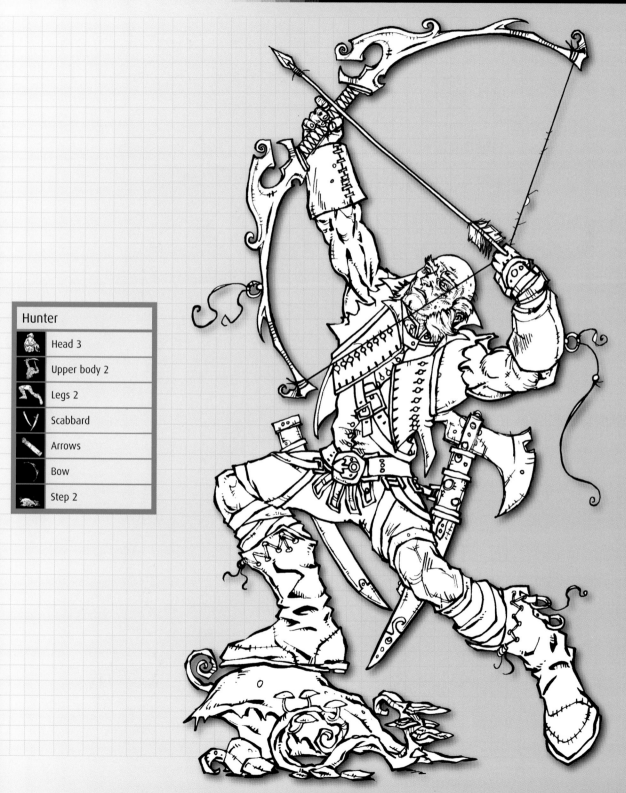

Hunter	
	Head 3
	Upper body 2
	Legs 2
	Scabbard
	Arrows
	Bow
	Step 2

FEMALE ADVENTURER 1

There are two different Female Adventurer files, named Female Adventurer 1 and Female Adventurer 2. Female Adventurer 1 has 19 layers, with two sets of legs and four bodies. The left and right arms are positioned above and below the body layers. Female Adventurer 2 is much simpler with just 11 layers arranged into legs and body layers. Both Female Adventurers have the same five head layers.

Fighter	
	Head 1
	Arm 4
	Body 2
	Legs 1
	Arm 2
	Staff
	Hair 2

Layers

	Head 5
	Head 4
	Head 3
	Head 2
	Head 1
	Arm 4
	Arm 3
	Body 4
	Body 3
	Body 2
	Body 1
	Legs 2
	Legs 1
	Arm 2
	Arm 1
	Bag
	Staff
	Hair 2
	Hair 1

Herbalist

	Head 2
	Arm 3
	Body 1
	Legs 2
	Arm 1
	Bag

FEMALE ADVENTURER 2

Layers

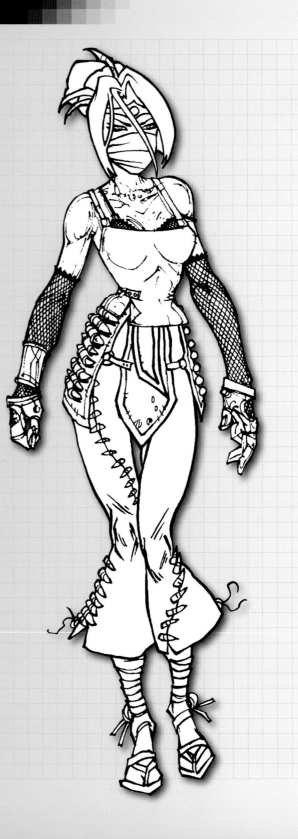	Head 5
	Head 4
	Head 3
	Head 2
	Head 1
	Body 3
	Body 2
	Body 1
	Legs 3
	Legs 2
	Legs 1

Assassin

	Head 4
	Body 3
	Legs 1

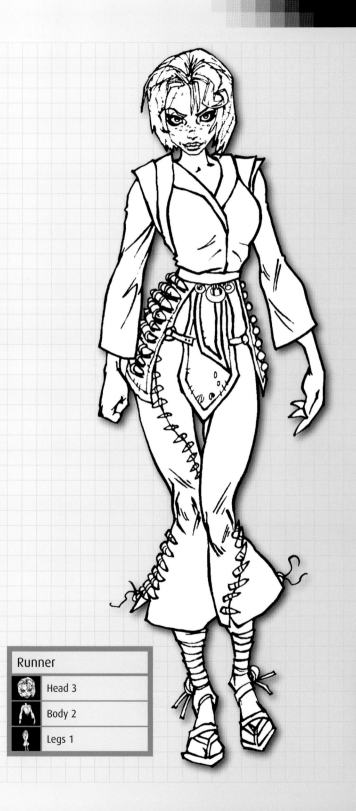

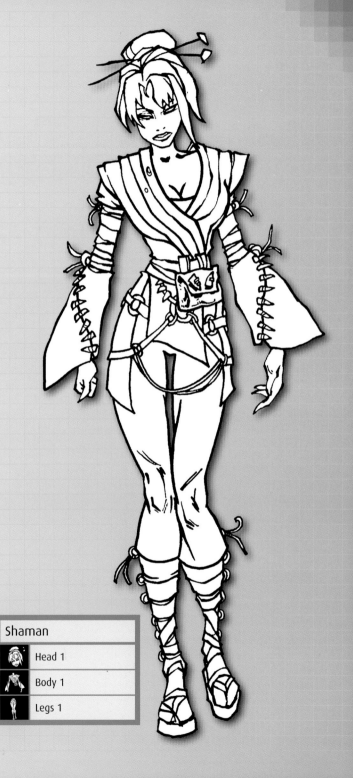

Runner

Head 3
Body 2
Legs 1

Shaman

Head 1
Body 1
Legs 1

MALE BARBARIAN 1

The are two different Male Barbarian files. Male Barbarian 1 has 14 layers and is relatively simple, with two sets of legs, four body layers with four heads, and three different weapons. Male Barbarian 2 has 20 layers, arranged in a logical order, with many more possible variations.

Brute	
	Weapon 1
	Head 7
	Body 2
	Legs 2

Layers

	Weapons
	Weapon 3
	Weapon 2
	Weapon 1
	Head 4
	Head 3
	Head 2
	Head 1
	Body 4
	Body 3
	Body 2
	Body 1
	Legs 2
	Legs 1

Skirmisher

	Weapon 3
	Head 3
	Body 1
	Legs 1

MALE BARBARIAN 2

Layers

	Weapons
	Head 6
	Head 5
	Head 4
	Head 3
	Head 2
	Head 1
	Sleeves
	Harness
	Shoulder guard 2
	Shoulder guard 1
	Torc
	Arms 3
	Arms 2
	Arms 1
	Belt 3
	Belt 2
	Belt 1
	Legs 1
	Midriff

Thug

	Head 5
	Harness
	Arms 2
	Belt 2
	Legs 1
	Midriff

Berserker

	Head 1
	Sleeves
	Torc
	Arms 1
	Belt 1
	Legs 1
	Midriff

Brawler

	Head 4
	Shoulder guard 1
	Arms 3
	Belt 1
	Legs 1
	Midriff

FEMALE BARBARIAN 1

There are two Female Barbarian files. Both share some features, such as legs, but each has unique body and head elements. Female Barbarian 1 has 18 layers, and care must be taken that your choice of weapon fits the figure exactly. Female Barbarian 2 also has 18 layers, but a simpler layer structure.

Sorceress	
	Head 1
	Body 3
	Legs 1
	Hair

Layers

	Head 3
	Head 2
	Head 1
	Glove
	Arm guard 2
	Arm guard 1
	Body 3
	Weapon 5
	Body 2
	Weapon 4
	Weapon 3
	Body 1
	Legs 3
	Legs 2
	Legs 1
	Weapon 2
	Weapon 1
	Hair

Unhinged

	Head 3
	Arm guard 1
	Body 2
	Weapon 3
	Legs 1
	Weapon 2

Night Fighter

	Head 2
	Glove
	Body 1
	Legs 2
	Weapon 1

FEMALE BARBARIAN 2

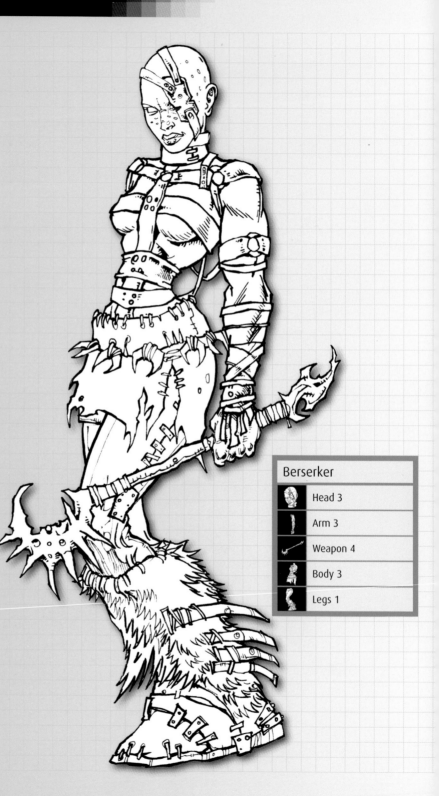

Layers

	Head 3
	Head 2
	Head 1
	Arm 3
	Arm 2
	Arm 1
	Weapon 6
	Weapon 5
	Weapon 4
	Weapon 3
	Body 3
	Body 2
	Body 1
	Legs 3
	Legs 2
	Legs 1
	Weapon 2
	Weapon 1

Berserker

	Head 3
	Arm 3
	Weapon 4
	Body 3
	Legs 1

Beast

	Head 2
	Arm 2
	Weapon 6
	Body 2
	Legs 2
	Weapon 2

Prize Fighter

	Head 1
	Arm 1
	Weapon 3
	Body 1
	Legs 3
	Weapon 1

WIZARD

The Wizard has 31 layers, offering a staggering number of possible variations. The arrangement of the layers is very simple, making it easy to choose from the different body, upper body, head, and arm layers to create your characters.

All-Seeing	
	Head 8
	Upper body 1
	Body 3
	Arms 3
	Collar 1

Layers

- Hat 3
- Hat 2
- Hat 1
- Head 10
- Head 9
- Head 8
- Head 7
- Head 6
- Head 5
- Head 4
- Head 3
- Head 2
- Head 1
- Upper body 3
- Upper body 2
- Upper body 1
- Body 3
- Belt 1
- Body 2
- Body 1
- Arms 4
- Arms 3
- Arms 2
- Arms 1

- Staff 5
- Staff 4
- Staff 3
- Staff 2
- Staff 1
- Collar 2
- Collar 1

Scheming

- Head 5
- Upper body 1
- Belt 1
- Body 1
- Arms 3
- Collar 2

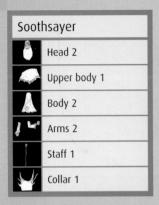

Soothsayer	
	Head 2
	Upper body 1
	Body 2
	Arms 2
	Staff 1
	Collar 1

Moody

	Hat 3
	Head 1
	Upper body 3
	Body 1
	Arms 1

In Two Minds

	Head 6
	Upper body 2
	Belt 1
	Body 2
	Arms 4

WITCH

With 28 layers, the Witch file has the potential to create every kind of hideous crone you could possibly dream up. The straightforward layout of the layers makes creation easy, enabling you to choose from the weapon, wand, arm, head, and body elements with ease. There are even three familiars to use too!

With Spider	
	Head 2
	Arms 1
	Broom
	Body 1
	Familiar 2

Layers

	Head 7
	Hat 4
	Hat 3
	Hat 2
	Hat 1
	Head 6
	Head 5
	Head 4
	Head 3
	Head 2
	Head 1
	Arms 5
	Arms 4
	Arms 3
	Arms 2
	Arms 1
	Wand 3
	Wand 2
	Wand 1
	Weapon 2
	Weapon 1
	Broom
	Body 3
	Body 2
	Body 1
	Familiar 3
	Familiar 2
	Familiar 1

Cyclops

Head 7
Arms 1
Weapon 1
Body 3

Scorpion

	Head 3
	Arms 5
	Body 2
	Familiar 3

Blind Warrior

	Hat 2
	Head 5
	Arms 4
	Body 3

With Cat	
	Hat 3
	Head 1
	Arms 3
	Body 3
	Familiar 1

MALE ELF

The Male Elf file has 25 layers in a slightly more complex arrangement, requiring a little care to ensure that the weapons correspond correctly with the upper body elements. The leg and head layers are more straightforward, and there are a number of accessories provided also.

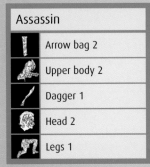

Assassin	
	Arrow bag 2
	Upper body 2
	Dagger 1
	Head 2
	Legs 1

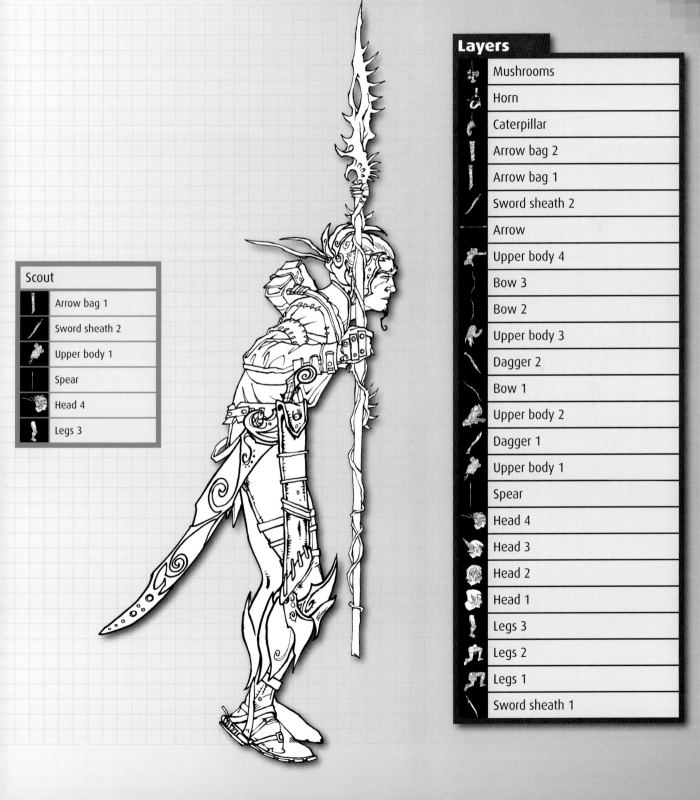

Scout

	Arrow bag 1
	Sword sheath 2
	Upper body 1
	Spear
	Head 4
	Legs 3

Layers

	Mushrooms
	Horn
	Caterpillar
	Arrow bag 2
	Arrow bag 1
	Sword sheath 2
	Arrow
	Upper body 4
	Bow 3
	Bow 2
	Upper body 3
	Dagger 2
	Bow 1
	Upper body 2
	Dagger 1
	Upper body 1
	Spear
	Head 4
	Head 3
	Head 2
	Head 1
	Legs 3
	Legs 2
	Legs 1
	Sword sheath 1

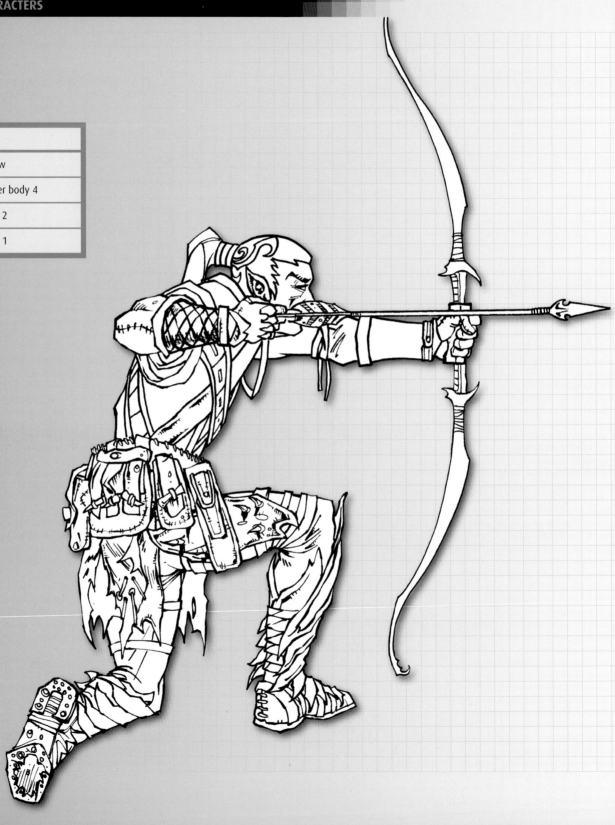

Archer

	Arrow
	Upper body 4
	Bow 2
	Legs 1

Gatherer

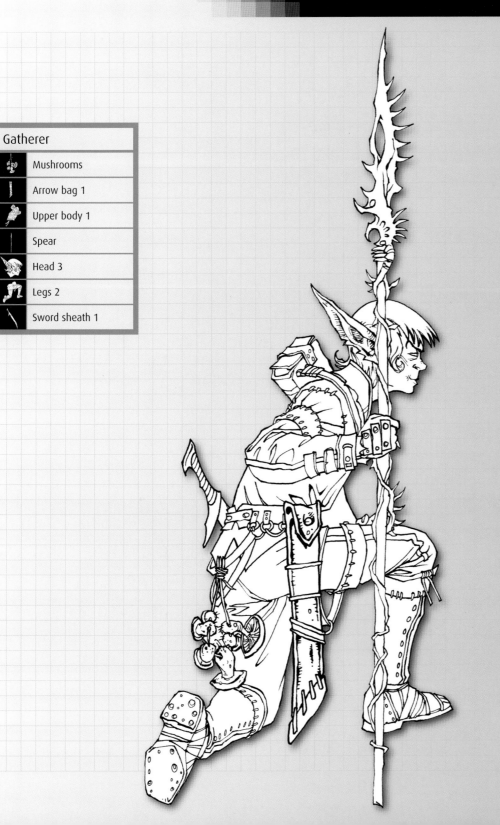	Mushrooms
	Arrow bag 1
	Upper body 1
	Spear
	Head 3
	Legs 2
	Sword sheath 1

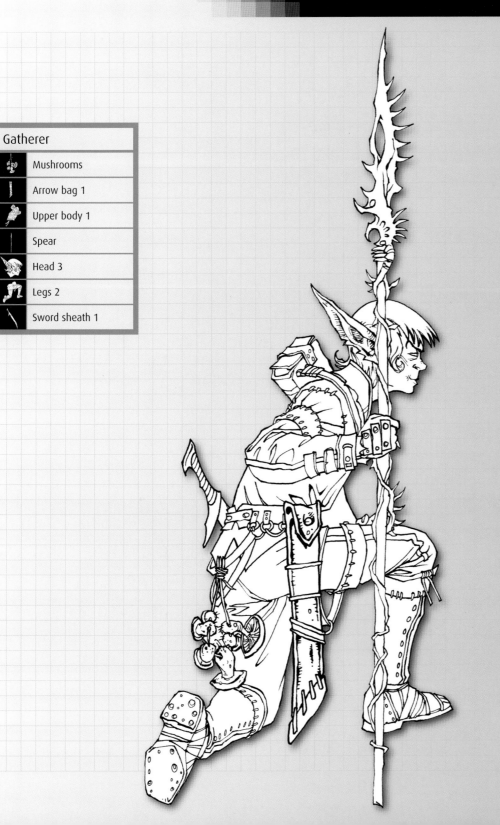

FEMALE ELF 1

The two Female Elf files are very easy to use, and each has its own specific characteristics. Female Elf 1 has 25 layers with weapons, hands, body, legs, and head elements grouped in sections. Female Elf 2 has 18 layers, with various specialized poses and features.

Warrior	
	Head 2
	Legs 3
	Body 2
	Hand 2
	Weapon 3

Layers

	Necklace
	Head 5
	Head 4
	Head 3
	Head 2
	Head 1
	Legs 4
	Legs 3
	Legs 2
	Legs 1
	Body 3
	Body 2
	Body 1
	Hand 4
	Hand 3
	Hand 2
	Hand 1
	Weapon 4
	Weapon 3
	Weapon 2
	Weapon 1
	Hair 2
	Hair 1
	Sash
	Quiver

Flail Fighter

	Head 1
	Legs 1
	Body 3
	Hand 2
	Weapon 2
	Hair 1

Duelist

	Head 5
	Legs 2
	Body 1
	Hand 3
	Weapon 4
	Sash

FEMALE ELF 2

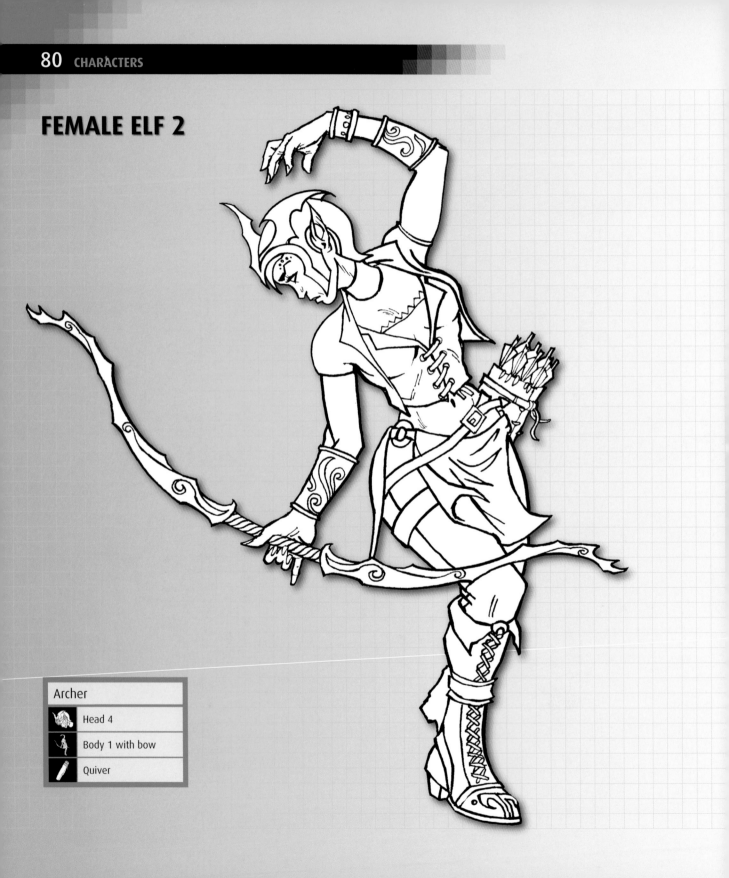

Archer	
	Head 4
	Body 1 with bow
	Quiver

Layers

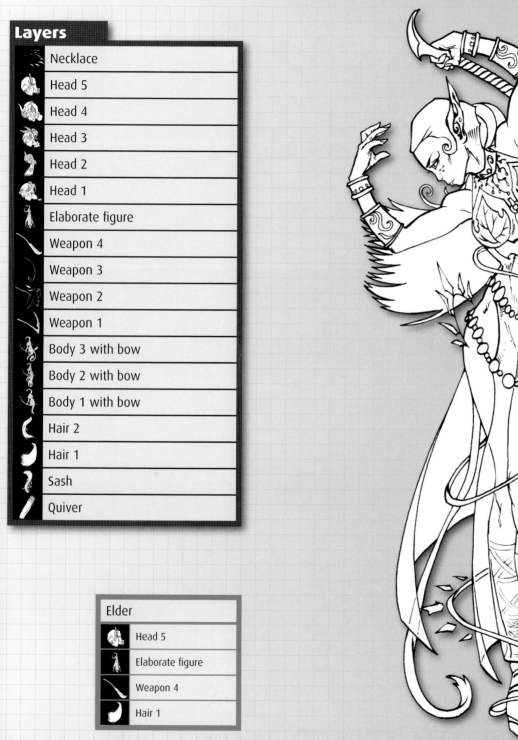

	Necklace
	Head 5
	Head 4
	Head 3
	Head 2
	Head 1
	Elaborate figure
	Weapon 4
	Weapon 3
	Weapon 2
	Weapon 1
	Body 3 with bow
	Body 2 with bow
	Body 1 with bow
	Hair 2
	Hair 1
	Sash
	Quiver

Elder

	Head 5
	Elaborate figure
	Weapon 4
	Hair 1

MALE DWARF

With 28 layers, the Male Dwarf file is a real heavyweight, but it is very simply arranged, enabling you to build a good gang of ready-to-work dwarves eager to plunder the nearest mountain of its buried wealth. Knowing their luck, however, they'll most likely dig up some ancient fiery demon before being chased off by hordes of Orcs, but it doesn't matter, you can always make some more!

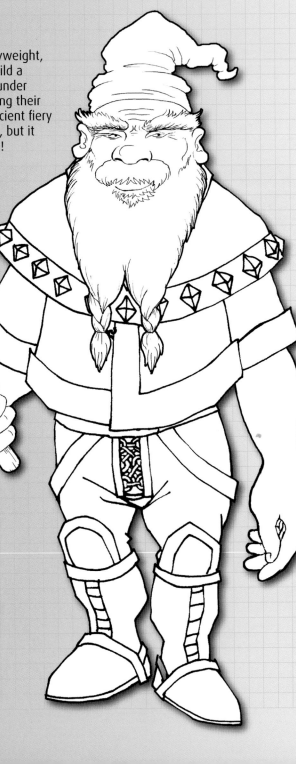

Dippy Doodle	
	Head 3
	Body 2
	Legs 2

Layers

	Head 11
	Head 10
	Head 9
	Head 8
	Head 7
	Head 6
	Head 5
	Head 4
	Head 3
	Head 2
	Head 1
	Hands 8
	Hands 7
	Hands 6
	Hands 5
	Hands 4
	Hands 3
	Hands 2
	Hands 1
	Shoulder armor
	Body 6
	Body 5
	Body 4
	Body 3
	Body 2
	Body 1
	Legs 2
	Legs 1

Thonk Nugshunk

	Head 11
	Body 3
	Legs 2

Cheery

	Head 2
	Hands 8
	Shoulder Armor
	Body 4
	Legs 1

Scodger

![head]	Head 8
![hands]	Hands 2
![body]	Body 6
![legs]	Legs 1

FEMALE DWARF

With 18 layers consisting of two hairstyles, six upper bodies, five bodies, and five heads, the Female Dwarf character file is concise, tidy, easy to interact with, and should result in some rewarding creations if treated with respect. Heck, you can even give her a beard if you like!

Battleaxe	
	Head 2
	Body 3
	Upper body 2
	Hair 2

Layers

	Head 5
	Head 4
	Head 3
	Head 2
	Head 1
	Body 5
	Body 4
	Body 3
	Body 2
	Body 1
	Upper body 6
	Upper body 5
	Upper body 4
	Upper body 3
	Upper body 2
	Upper body 1
	Hair 2
	Hair 1

Kute

	Head 1
	Body 1
	Upper body 1
	Hair 1

Betty

	Head 5
	Body 5
	Upper body 6

Grushnilga

Head 3

Body 2

Upper body 4

MALE CHILD

The Male Child file is simply laid out with 17 layers. The possibilities of this character include creatures such as halflings or imps, and it shouldn't be too hard to create a whole village full of the little scamps!

Halfling

	Head 1
	Legs 1
	Torso

Layers

	Head 5
	Head 4
	Head 3
	Head 2
	Head 1
	Neck leaves
	Belt 3
	Belt 2
	Belt 1
	Shoes
	Legs 3
	Legs 2
	Legs 1
	Bracers
	Shirt 2
	Shirt 1
	Torso

Imp

	Head 4
	Neck leaves
	Shoes
	Legs 3
	Bracers
	Shirt 1
	Torso

Thief	
	Head 5
	Belt 1
	Legs 1
	Shirt 1
	Torso

Scampler	
	Head 3
	Legs 2
	Shirt 2
	Torso

FEMALE CHILD

The Female Child file has 22 layers set out in a very straightforward arrangement of wings, body elements, and assorted appendages. She is well suited to the creation of Fairies and other such creatures, so the bottom of your garden need never be lonely again!

Weird Fairy	
	Head 4
	Legs 2
	Torso 3
	Appendage 4
	Appendage 3
	Appendage 2
	Appendage 1

Crazy Fairy	
	Head 6
	Legs 1
	Torso 1
	Appendage 3
	Wings 4

Fairy

	Head 1
	Legs 1
	Torso 1
	Wings 3

Layers

	Head 7
	Head 6
	Head 5
	Head 4
	Head 3
	Head 2
	Head 1
	Hair
	Legs 2
	Foot wing
	Legs 1
	Torso 3
	Torso 2
	Torso 1
	Appendage 4
	Appendage 3
	Appendage 2
	Appendage 1
	Wings 4
	Wings 3
	Wings 2
	Wings 1

Scary Fairy

	Head 2
	Hair
	Foot wing
	Legs 1
	Torso 2
	Appendage 4
	Wings 2

HORSEMAN

The Horseman is another very easy-to-use file with 19 layers arranged in logical sections. Just choose a horse rear, a rider, and a horse front, and your cavalry is well on the way to creation!

Layers

	Horse front 6
	Horse front 5
	Horse front 4
	Horse front 3
	Horse front 2
	Horse front 1
	Rider 7
	Rider 6
	Rider 5
	Rider 4
	Rider 3
	Rider 2
	Rider 1
	Horse rear 4
	Horse rear 3
	Horse rear 2
	Horse rear 1
	War paint
	Bareback warrior

Skirmisher	
	Horse front 4
	Rider 1
	Horse rear 2

Death Knight

	Horse front 2
	Rider 7
	Horse rear 2

Champion

	Horse front 5
	Rider 3
	Horse rear 4

Skelnash

	Horse front 1
	Rider 4
	Horse rear 1

HORSEWOMAN

The Horsewoman file has 20 layers, and she is perhaps one of the easiest to get to grips with—but don't tell her I said that! The horse, saddle, rider, and shield elements are arranged in an intuitive order, so dive in and see what you can come up with!

Layers

	Rider 7
	Shield 4
	Shield 3
	Rider 6
	Rider 5
	Rider 4
	Rider 3
	Shield 2
	Shield 1
	Rider 2
	Rider 1
	Saddle 3
	Saddle 2
	Saddle 1
	Horse 6
	Horse 5
	Horse 4
	Horse 3
	Horse 2
	Horse 1

Tentakill

	Rider 7
	Saddle 3
	Horse 3

Boudica

	Rider 1
	Saddle 2
	Horse 1

Spear Maiden

	Shield 3
	Rider 3
	Saddle 1
	Horse 4

Centauria

	Shield 4
	Saddle 1
	Horse 2

ORC 1

With not one, but two different Orc files on the disc, you have everything you need to breed your own hideous army in the caverns beneath your tower. Or in your computer at the very least. Orc 1 has 26 layers, while Orc 2 has 19. Each file is laid out in an unusually organized way for an Orc, making the task of fitting the coolest head to the ugliest body that much easier. However, you might like to think twice before giving your Orc-ish creations legs, as it might just encourage them to rampage all over your desktop. Orcs . . . what can you do?

Knife Fighter	
	Head 4
	Shield 3
	Armor
	Belt 2
	Body 4
	Weapon 4
	Leg wear 3
	Leg wear 2
	Legs

Layers

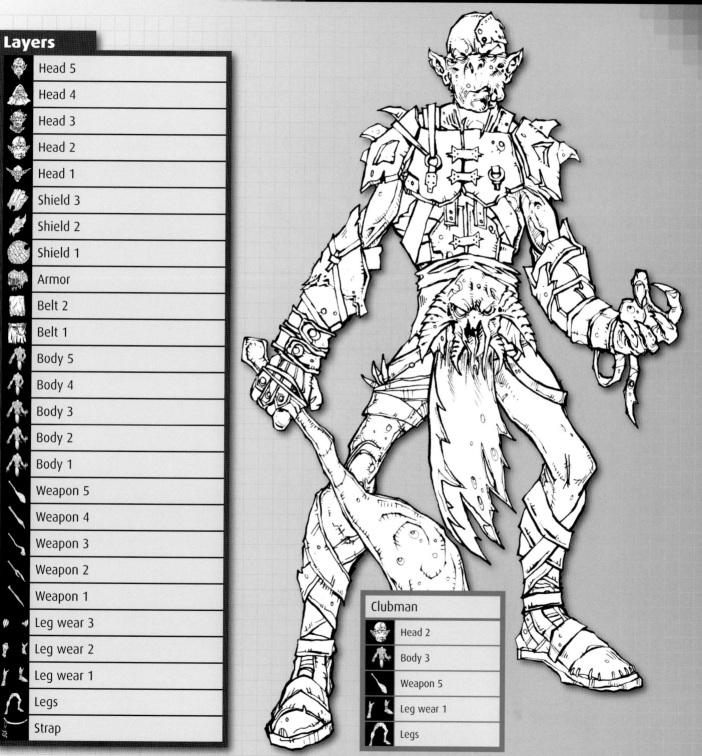

- Head 5
- Head 4
- Head 3
- Head 2
- Head 1
- Shield 3
- Shield 2
- Shield 1
- Armor
- Belt 2
- Belt 1
- Body 5
- Body 4
- Body 3
- Body 2
- Body 1
- Weapon 5
- Weapon 4
- Weapon 3
- Weapon 2
- Weapon 1
- Leg wear 3
- Leg wear 2
- Leg wear 1
- Legs
- Strap

Clubman

- Head 2
- Body 3
- Weapon 5
- Leg wear 1
- Legs

ORC 2

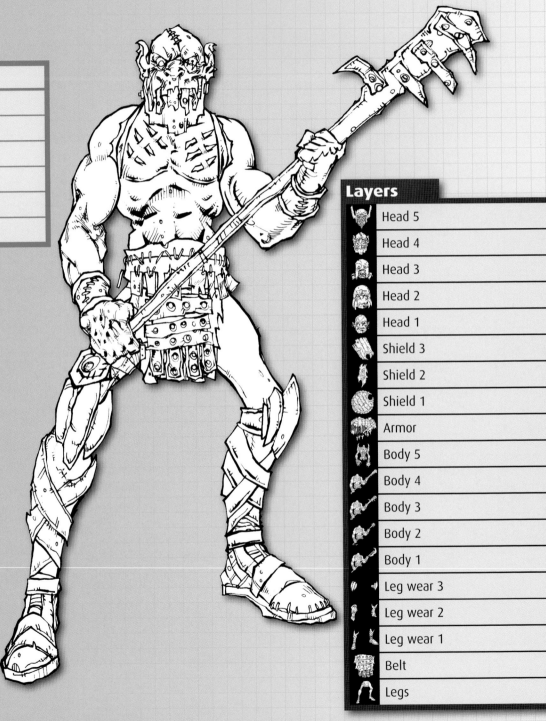

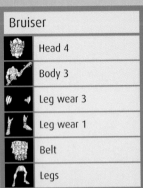

Bruiser	
	Head 4
	Body 3
	Leg wear 3
	Leg wear 1
	Belt
	Legs

Layers

	Head 5
	Head 4
	Head 3
	Head 2
	Head 1
	Shield 3
	Shield 2
	Shield 1
	Armor
	Body 5
	Body 4
	Body 3
	Body 2
	Body 1
	Leg wear 3
	Leg wear 2
	Leg wear 1
	Belt
	Legs

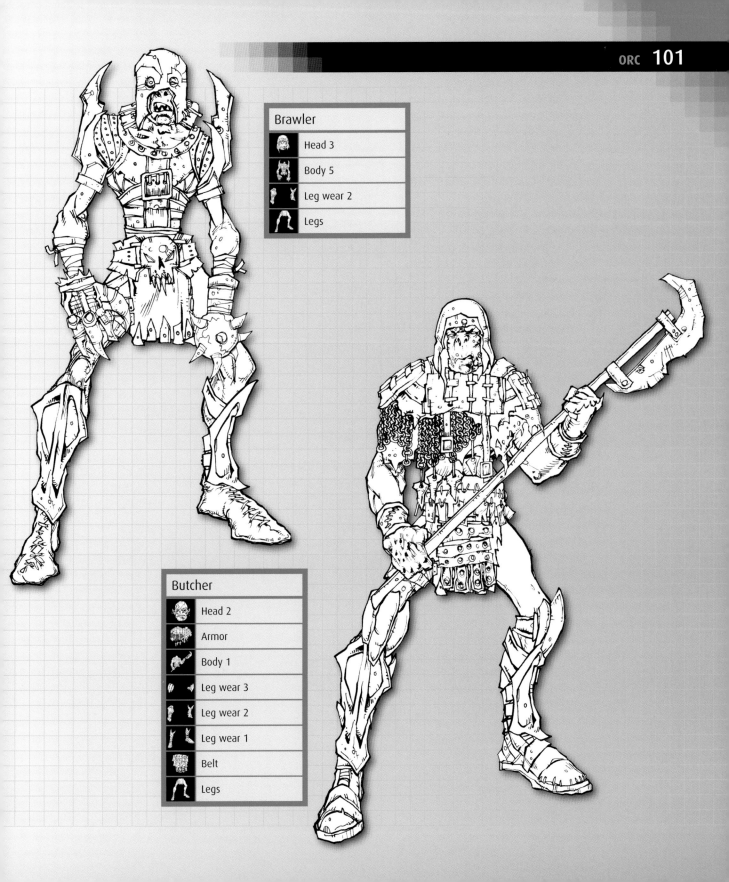

Brawler

	Head 3
	Body 5
	Leg wear 2
	Legs

Butcher

	Head 2
	Armor
	Body 1
	Leg wear 3
	Leg wear 2
	Leg wear 1
	Belt
	Legs

OGRE

The Ogre is a very simple file with 20 layers arranged in an easy-to-use way. Even so, there are enough heads, weapons, and accessories to create a broad range of hulking creatures, none of which are very pretty.

Abrute	
	Head 1
	Forearm bracers
	Belt 1
	Body
	Weapon 1
	Legs

Abomination

	Head 5
	Shoulder armor
	Forearm bracers
	Body
	Weapon 2
	Legs

Layers

	Head 6
	Head 5
	Head 4
	Head 3
	Head 2
	Head 1
	Shoulder armor
	Forearm bracers
	Harness
	Belt 2
	Belt 1
	Shirt
	Body
	Weapon 5
	Weapon 4
	Weapon 3
	Weapon 2
	Weapon 1
	Footwear
	Legs

Prize Fighter

	Head 6
	Shoulder armor
	Forearm bracers
	Harness
	Belt 1
	Shirt
	Body
	Weapon 5
	Footwear
	Legs

Thug	
	Head 4
	Harness
	Belt 1
	Body
	Weapon 4
	Footwear
	Legs

Skull Collector	
	Head 3
	Belt 2
	Shirt
	Body
	Weapon 3
	Footwear
	Legs

HORSE

The Horse file features 21 fun layers, ten of which are the most fabulous collection of equine heads you've ever seen. You're guaranteed to win any race riding an animal put together using this file; all the other competitors will be too scared to leave their boxes! Unless you choose to pick the slow coach layer . . . Puzzled? Better check out the file then!

Centaur	
	Centaur
	Leg guards
	Body

Layers	
	Slow coach
	Centaur
	Horn 2
	Horn 1
	Saddle 3
	Saddle 2
	Saddle 1
	Blanket
	Head 10
	Head 9
	Head 8
	Head 7
	Head 6
	Head 5
	Head 4
	Head 3
	Head 2
	Head 1
	Extra leg
	Leg guards
	Body

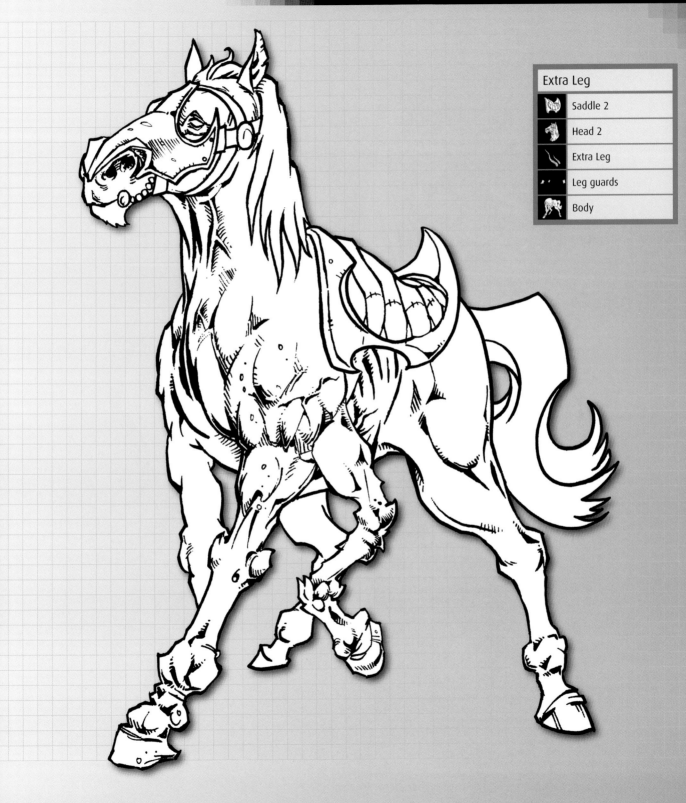

	Extra Leg
	Saddle 2
	Head 2
	Extra Leg
	Leg guards
	Body

Horns	
	Horn 2
	Saddle 3
	Head 1
	Leg guards
	Body

Tentacles

	Head 6
	Body

Leechhead

	Head 8
	Leg guards
	Body

DRAGON

The Dragon—the character you've all been waiting for. Well, we hope this 10-headed beast doesn't disappoint! With 20 layers of sulphur-soaked, serpentine terror at your disposal, it's frightening to imagine what you might cook up.

Layers

	Arms 2
	Arms 1
	Head 10
	Head 9
	Head 8
	Head 7
	Head 6
	Head 5
	Head 4
	Head 3
	Head 2
	Head 1
	Dragon body 1
	Appendage 4
	Appendage 3
	Appendage 2
	Appendage 1
	Wings 3
	Wings 2
	Wings 1

Armored

	Arms 2
	Head 3
	Dragon Body 1
	Wings 1

Mutated

	Arms 2
	Head 10
	Dragon body 1
	Appendage 4

Two Heads

	Arms 1
	Head 9
	Dragon body 1

Lord	
	Arms 1
	Head 1
	Dragon body 1
	Appendage 4
	Wings 2

Beast

	Arms 2
	Head 7
	Dragon body 1
	Appendage 3
	Wings 3

MONSTER

Nothing can prepare you for the rapturous revulsion that awaits in the form of this 18-layer Monster file, featuring multiple heads, grisly appendages that defy medical classification, and other parts too deliciously disturbing to even think about. There is bound to be something here to get even the thickest-skinned monster-phile yelping in gleeful terror!

Nightmare	
	Head 7
	Lower body 3
	Upper body 1

Worm

	Head 3
	Appendage 1
	Lower body 3
	Upper body 1

Layers

	Upper body 3
	Appendage 4
	Appendage 3
	Head 8
	Head 7
	Head 6
	Head 5
	Head 4
	Head 3
	Head 2
	Head 1
	Appendage 2
	Appendage 1
	Lower body 3
	Upper body 2
	Lower body 2
	Lower body 1
	Upper body 1

Lizard	
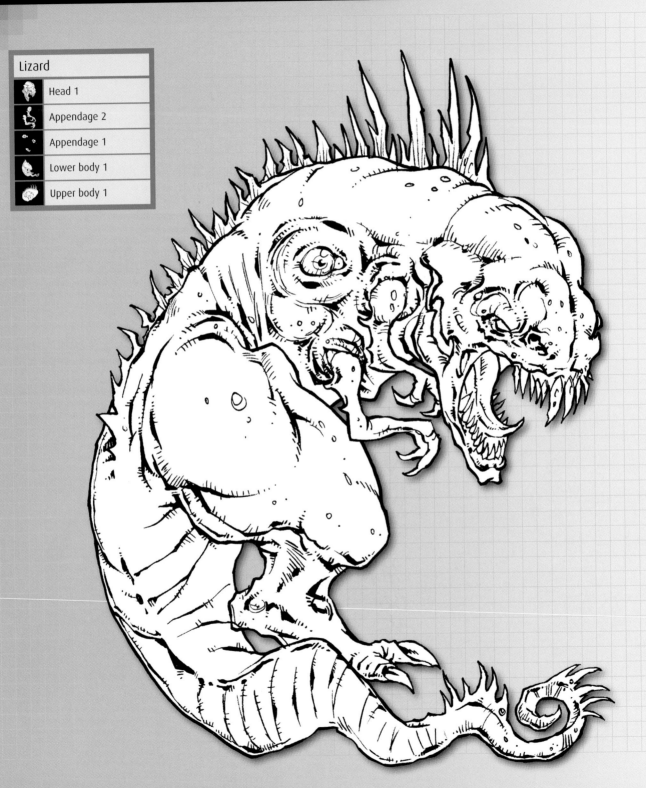	Head 1
	Appendage 2
	Appendage 1
	Lower body 1
	Upper body 1

Mantis

	Head 4
	Upper body 2
	Lower body 2

TROLL

With 22 layers, the Troll is an imposing character, packed with countless variations on the theme of big, dumb creatures with big, scary clubs. And swords. And other implements used for squishing other things. The only thing missing is a bridge for them to hide beneath, but we hope you have a good time "trolling" through the file anyway.

Cyclops	
	Head 9
	Body 2
	Weapon 5
	Legs 2

Layers

	Head 9
	Head 8
	Head 7
	Head 6
	Head 5
	Head 4
	Head 3
	Head 2
	Head 1
	Body 4
	Body 3
	Body 2
	Body 1
	Weapon 6
	Weapon 5
	Weapon 4
	Weapon 3
	Weapon 2
	Weapon 1
	Legs 3
	Legs 2
	Legs 1

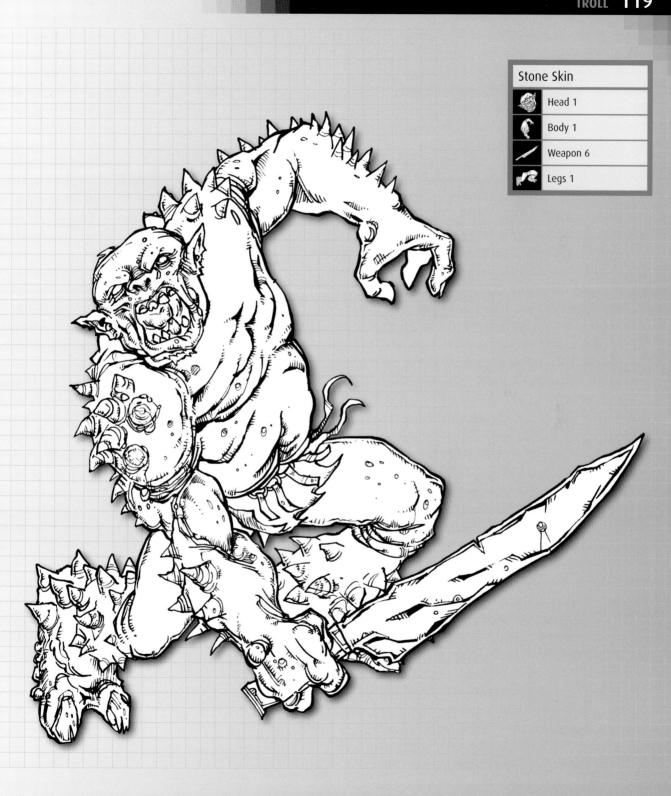

Stone Skin	
Head	1
Body	1
Weapon	6
Legs	1

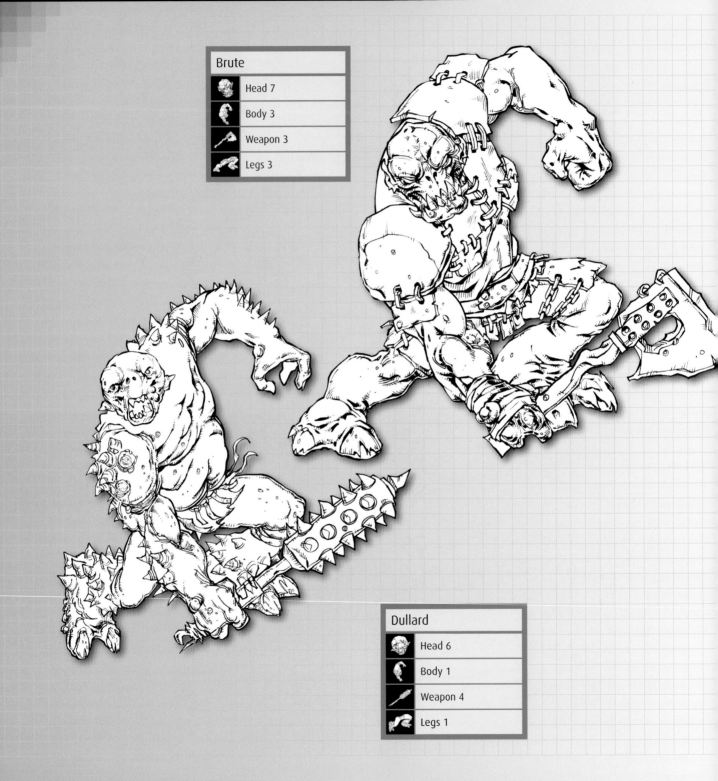

Brute

	Head 7
	Body 3
	Weapon 3
	Legs 3

Dullard

	Head 6
	Body 1
	Weapon 4
	Legs 1

Cave Dweller

Head 3

Body 2

Weapon 2

Legs 2

BACKGROUNDS

Mountains 1 and 2
The two Mountain
backgrounds depict wild,
untamed environments.
The mountain elements
create a feeling of distance
and intrigue, perfect for
the Adventurer characters.

Ruined Temple

The Ruined Temple background represents a failed attempt to construct a building amid vicious fangs of rock on a stone plinth at their summit. Just the sort of place you might find a Wizard or Witch—or if you're really unlucky, a Dragon!

Stone Fangs

This hostile environment would make a fine home for an Orc, if he could avoid being eaten by the Monsters and Dragons that would also live here!

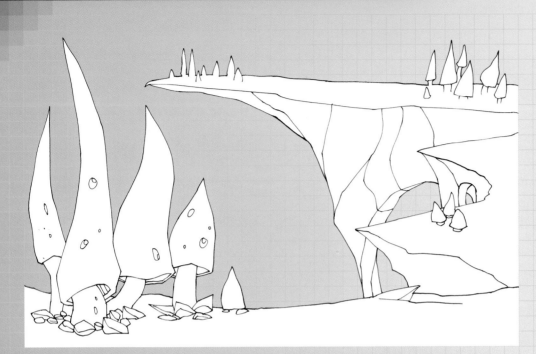

Spike Fungi
With unfriendly fungi this large, only the most fearless or foolhardy character would attempt to eat them. That'll be the Ogre then!

Striped Boulders
This background is rather more friendly than some of the others. With its striped, curved boulders and spectacular rock formations in the distance, any number of characters might be seen wandering around here!

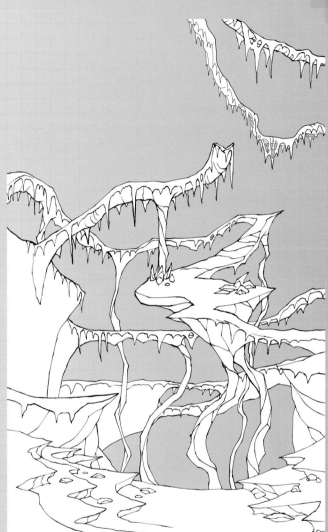

Sundials
This background is very eye-catching and ethereal in its formation. Fairies might well be expected to flutter between the towering spires . . . but other things with wings might also be attracted to their heights.

Twisting Walkways
In such an extreme environment, with mazes of walkways suspended in space, only the most surefooted would dare to walk here. Yet such treacherous structures hold no fear for Elf kind . . .

ACCESSORIES

There is a huge range of possible accessories to choose from, neatly contained within four files. You can browse them here, or open, say, the Axes and Clubs file, then browse the layers onscreen. Pick your favorite and drag it across to your character just as described on page 21.

Axes & Clubs

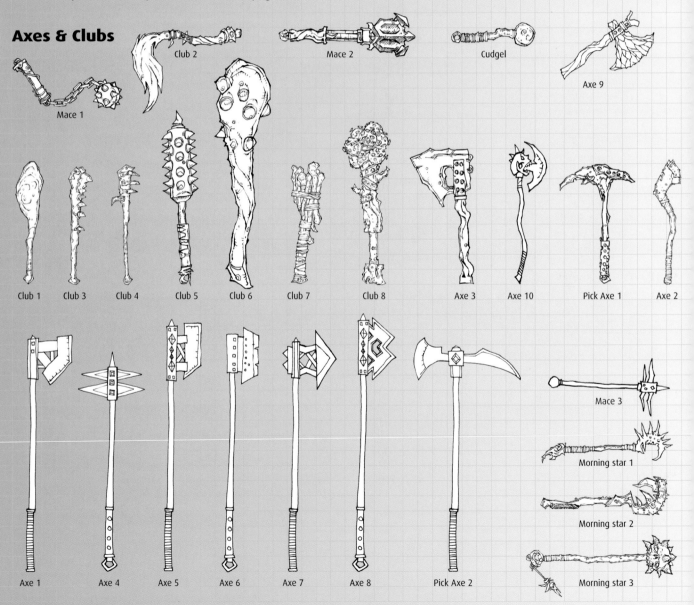

Club 2

Mace 2

Cudgel

Axe 9

Mace 1

Club 1 Club 3 Club 4 Club 5 Club 6 Club 7 Club 8 Axe 3 Axe 10 Pick Axe 1 Axe 2

Axe 1 Axe 4 Axe 5 Axe 6 Axe 7 Axe 8 Pick Axe 2

Mace 3

Morning star 1

Morning star 2

Morning star 3

Spears & Bows

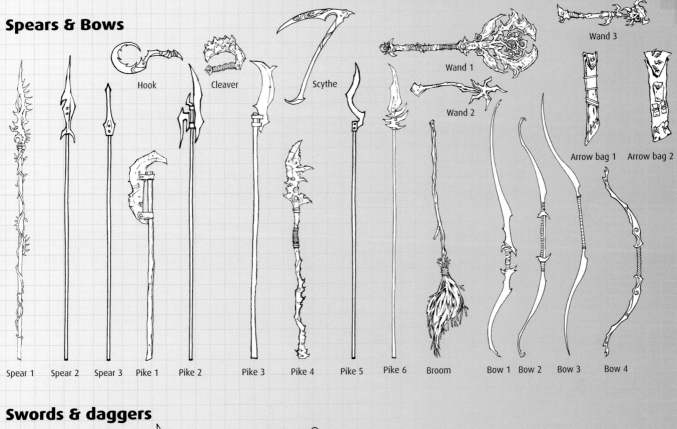

Hook

Cleaver

Scythe

Wand 1

Wand 2

Wand 3

Arrow bag 1   Arrow bag 2

Spear 1   Spear 2   Spear 3   Pike 1   Pike 2   Pike 3   Pike 4   Pike 5   Pike 6   Broom   Bow 1   Bow 2   Bow 3   Bow 4

Swords & daggers

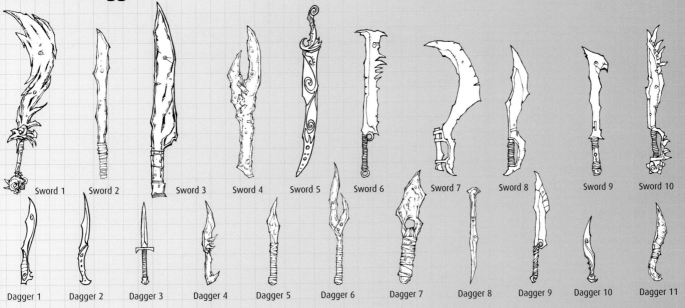

Sword 1   Sword 2   Sword 3   Sword 4   Sword 5   Sword 6   Sword 7   Sword 8   Sword 9   Sword 10

Dagger 1   Dagger 2   Dagger 3   Dagger 4   Dagger 5   Dagger 6   Dagger 7   Dagger 8   Dagger 9   Dagger 10   Dagger 11

Various

Helm 2

Helm 3

Helm 1

Skull cap

Hood

Shield 2

Worm

Helm 4

Skull

Bag 1

Bag 3

Bag 2

Armor

Shield 1

AGILITY		7
STAMINA		8
STRENGTH		7
HIT POINTS		6

Card game

As a little treat, we've also thrown in a blank game card that you can use to make any game you wish. Simply drop your character into the Layers palette, beneath everything except the Background layer.

The card is fully customizable, allowing you to type your own text into any of the fields, not just the "points" boxes. There are also some Hue/Saturation adjustment layers, so if you want to change the color scheme, just double-click and move the slider—you'll be done in seconds.

Finally, print off your cards onto stiff photo-quality paper for a professional feel, and invite your friends over to play. Not only will they love your creations, but since you made up the rules, you'll always win as well!